The Poems of Meleager

The Poems of
MELEAGER

Verse translations by Peter Whigham
Introduction and literal translations
　by Peter Jay

University of California Press
Berkeley and Los Angeles

University of California Press
Berkeley and Los Angeles, California

ISBN: 0-520-03003-6
Library of Congress Catalog Card Number: 75-7196

Verse translations copyright © Peter Whigham 1975
All other material copyright © Peter Jay 1975

Contents

Introduction

THE POEMS OF MELEAGER – Greek texts
   and versions by Peter Whigham

Literal Translations and Notes
Appendix – The Poem on Spring, the Preface
   and Epilogue to the *Garland*
A Note on Garlands, Symposia and the Komos
Select Bibliography

Note

The Greek texts printed are those of A. S. F. Gow and D. L. Page in *Hellenistic Epigrams* (1965), vol. 1, except for poem 57 and the first poem in the Appendix (both omitted by Gow and Page) which follow W. R. Paton's Loeb text. For permission to reproduce their Greek texts, and for the quotations from their commentary in vol. 2 of *Hellenistic Epigrams*, we thank the authors and the Cambridge University Press. We are also grateful to the Cambridge University Press for permission to quote the passage from Walter Headlam's commentary in *The Mimes of Herodas*, edited by A. D. Knox (1924).

Introduction

Meleager (the Greek form is Meleagros), son of Eukratēs, was born in about 140 BC at Gadara, a town just south of the eastern shore of the Sea of Galilee.[1] He grew up and was educated at Tyre, the ancient Phoenician coastal city, but spent his later life on Kos, the island off the Karian south-west corner of Asia Minor. He died in old age, probably about 70 BC. He wrote poetry, popular philosophical essays which he called *Charites* (Graces) in a mixture of prose and verse, and edited an important collection of Greek epigrams known as the *Garland*.

All this can be gathered from Meleager's four autobiographical poems, two of which are included in this selection (poems 57 and 58). While it is not much to go by, it is more than is known about many Greek poets, although in Meleager's case, the information does not add substantially to one's appreciation of the poems.

A little more can be inferred about his background. Gadara was a Hellenic town, whose Greek-speaking society survived into the Christian era. Meleager's parents were certainly of this well-to-do class, even if by origin they were part-Syrian. Meleager was in all probability bilingual, but little that is recognisably Syrian comes through into the poems; however it is arguable, if unprovable, that Meleager's temperament and stylistic propensities are Syrian at root rather than Greek. The poem about spring[2] perhaps owes something to the landscape of his homeland and even to its folk-poetry (passages of *The Song of Songs* are a little similar) – but it also recalls the pastoral reliefs of Hellenistic art. It is at least a harmless supposition that Meleager, whose intellectual curiosity led him to make a critical anthology of Greek epigram, was neither wholly ignorant of, nor uninfluenced by his homeland's cultural traditions.

Meleager compiled the *Garland* on Kos, an island with a literary tradition of its own, where the third-century BC poets Philitas and Theokritos had lived. Anthologies of epigram had been made before, but the survival of Meleager's at least until the tenth century AD, when the Byzantine Kephalas incorporated its poems into The Palatine Anthology[3], implies that it was one of the best. On balance, the evidence suggests that Meleager compiled his anthology in the early years of the first century BC.[4] It was an extensive collection, containing perhaps 4,000 lines of verse. Meleager's prefatory poem, though not a complete list of the poets included, gives a good idea of its range. Although the *Garland* concentrated on the poets of the third century, when epigram really came into its own, Meleager also included a large number – perhaps all – the epigrams by earlier poets available to him; there were epigrams from the seventh century (Archilochos) to his own day. Whether he published a separate collection of his own poems is not known; it seems unlikely, since he certainly included the bulk of his verse in the *Garland*.

The Palatine Anthology does not, perhaps, include every poem of Meleager's *Garland*, but it is clear that there are stretches of poems which Kephalas has lifted wholesale from it. These show that Meleager arranged the poems not by author, but by theme, often alternating between the principal poets in each section, and capping a sequence of earlier poems with one of his own.[5] Meleager's editing and arrangement of the *Garland* make it obvious that he enjoyed an intimate knowledge of all aspects of Greek epigram; that he was conscious both of his place in the tradition, and of his ability to renew and extend it. The scope of Greek epigram, which originally meant a formal verse inscription – usually an epitaph or dedication to a god – had been greatly widened by the early Hellenistic poets such as Asklepiades, so that it became a vehicle for most types of short, personal or public poem, encompassing some areas which we would now loosely term 'lyric'.[6] Meleager was especially fond of capping poems by the two poets with whom he has most in common, Asklepiades and Kallimachos. When he does so, his poem always contains some new combination of motifs, some new refinement to distinguish it from mere imitation. Meleager's originality as a poet lies very much in his inventiveness in combining and adapting old themes into new entities. In doing so he transforms and enlivens the whole genre.

Meleager could write equally well with elegant restraint and simplicity, or else with flamboyant elaboration and clever coining of novel compound words. If Coleridge's dictum that poetry is 'the best words in the best order' may be applied anachronistically, Meleager fulfils its terms by exploiting all the natural advantages of his inflected language. The variety of styles he could handle gives his work an air of continuous experiment; he never liked to do the same thing twice.

Meleager has sometimes struck critics as too ingenious to be sincere. Gow and Page, for example, seem to adopt a sincerity-of-emotion standard for poetry and question the effectiveness of poem 53 because it seems too consciously composed to be heartfelt. In their preface to Meleager's poems, they write:

> The limitations both of matter and of form which he inherited, and which he accepted without question, are such that it seems to us a misunderstanding of the essential nature of his work to call him a 'real poet', or to look for anything 'fresh with joyous experience' [J. A. Symonds' descriptions]. It is hard to say in what literary form a poet of this period (or for long before) would have expressed the profounder personal emotions. Certainly it would not have been the epigram, in which poetry had long been degenerating into a parlour-game.... The epigram was a field rather for exercise of the intellect than for display of the emotions.... It may be admitted that a glimmer of true emotion can be discerned here and there, but it is quite certain that most of the light is artificial.

What mode, then, should a 'real poet' have chosen? Meleager's seems perfectly legitimate to me; there was no alternative but to revive and renew the tradition of epigram. A little later, Catullus found epigram to be the right form for poems which unquestionably concern the 'profounder personal emotions'. How, indeed if, emotional sincerity can ever be measured is another problem; it cannot be the primary test of a 'real poet', for many bad poets have been emotionally sincere.

One should in any case distinguish between ancient and modern notions of the relationship between art and life. When reading Greek poets one should not assume that the *persona* or speaker of the poem is necessarily the poet himself; there is a long tradition of impersonal poetry. This is not to say that Meleager's poems are untrue to his feelings; simply that expression of his own emotions is not the purpose of the poems. It would be quite wrong to call Meleager an 'academic' or literary poet merely because he frequently adapts poems by Asklepiades and Kallimachos; this was expected of an epigrammatist. Besides, Meleager's poems are too palpably alive as poems to merit the adjective 'literary' in its derogatory sense. The relationship between his art and his life remains unclear, but we may be sure that Meleager was too good a poet to publish work merely because his 'real' feelings of sexual delectation, frustration etc., had been expressed in a poem.

Meleager's poetic authenticity lies in the mastery of every aspect of his medium. He used every mode of epigram and most combinations of them: dedicatory, epideictic (descriptive), epitaphic or sepulchral, sympotic and erotic. It is as a love-poet, the area which he most developed, that he is supremely the best of Greek epigrammatists. He employs the whole range of traditional erotic imagery and rings all the changes on it. He is the first poet to give Eros the role which has become so familiar to us in love-poetry.

It would be otiose to give here any detailed account of Meleager's style and technique. It is, however, worth noting his sureness of touch with what Pound termed *logopoeia* – the modulated tone of his language, now direct and simple, now ironic, or allusive: this is a major feature of Meleager's technique, and failure to recognize the different 'voices' – to distinguish poems like 33, for example, from 55 – would be to miss much of the real poetry. Meleager's imagery is to a great extent connected with the conventions of sympotic poetry, on which see the 'Note on Garlands, Symposia and the Kōmos'; but his use of the imagery of flowers is nevertheless peculiar to himself, and the imagery of light is also very much his own.

Meleager's essays are lost. There are two quotations surviving in Athenaios' miscellany, the *Deipnosophistai*; both short enough to quote here. 'Nikion said, "Do none of you . . . eat fish? Or is it like what your ancestor Meleager of Gadara, in the work called *Charites*, said of Homer: that being a Syrian by birth, he accordingly represented the Achaians as abstaining from fish, in keeping with the Syrian practice, though there is an abundance of fish around the Hellespont?" ' [Ath. 4.157b]. Discussing the word *chytridēs* (jug, pot): 'The Cynic Meleager also quotes the word, writing this in his *Symposion* – "and at this juncture, he assigned to him a heavy task – twelve deep pots (*chytridia*)".' [Ath. 11.502c].

Charites was a collection of miscellaneous essays on philosophical topics, in the form which, through Varro's adaptations, the Romans knew as 'Menippean satire'. In this Meleager followed another Gadarene writer, the third-century Cynic Menippos, who developed this serio-comic style in a mixture of prose and verse for his philosophical essays. Meleager has an important place in literary history as the second main writer in this branch of belles-lettres, but his contribution to it is of course unclear.

In the absence of his *Charites* it is hard to guess what influence his Cynicism had on his poetry. Cynicism was never an organized philosophical school in the way that Epicureanism was; individual Cynics interpreted the principles of Diogenes in their own way. The basic ideal was to lead a simple and self-sufficient (but not necessarily ascetic) life, free from the troubles brought by material possessions. It was very much an apolitical, individualist philosophy, and as such is quite compatible with Meleager's *persona* in the poems, which affirm the values of the individual's personal life, almost divorced from the wider social context. The argument from silence should not be pressed beyond this, and perhaps one should say no more than that Meleager's values (in common with the majority of Hellenistic epigrammatists) were very different from, say, the values and concepts of Greek nationhood which informed the poems of Simonides at the time of the wars with Persia.

Meleager's *Garland* was an influential book. Catullus and the Roman elegists had absorbed it, much as English and American poets have absorbed the pioneering modernist poetry of the 1910s and 1920s. Later epigrammatists writing in Greek tended to avoid erotic epigram, perhaps on the grounds that Meleager had temporarily exhausted its possibilities. (One of the few exceptions to this rule is Meleager's compatriot, Philodemos of Gadara, some thirty years younger than Meleager; he began writing too late to be included in the *Garland*.) Erotic epigram was briefly revived in the sixth century AD with Paulos and the early Byzantine poets. Many of Meleager's themes and some of his spirit has filtered through into English poetry, via such poets as Herrick, who imitated and adapted a few of his poems.

This selection contains a little under half of Meleager's surviving verse; it includes all his best and most characteristic poems. The arrangement of the poems (Poems 1–6, Kypris and Eros; 7–19, homosexual poems; 20–33, miscellaneous heterosexual poems; 34–41, poems to Zenophile; 42–53, poems to Heliodora; 54–58, miscellaneous) is meant to be no more than orderly: it should not be read as any kind of pseudo-biographical sequence, nor is it likely to reflect any possible order of composition.

My literal versions were made independently of Peter Whigham's verse translations. I should like to express my debt to Mr A. S. F. Gow and Prof. Sir Denys Page, whose commentary on Meleager has been invaluable in the preparation of the literal versions and notes.

PETER JAY

[1]Not the coastal Gadara near Askalon – see H. Ouvré, *Méléagre de Gadara*, chapter 1.

[2]Possibly an early piece: it is his only poem in a metre (the hexameter) other than the elegiac couplet. The text and prose translation are given in the Appendix.

[3]The Palatine Anthology forms the first fifteen books of modern editions of The Greek Anthology. Book 16 is an appendix of poems omitted by Kephalas but included by Planudes, who re-edited the collection in 1301.

[4]A marginal note to the Palatine ms. gives Meleager's *floruit* as 'the reign of the last Seleukos' (96–5 BC).

[5]For a discussion of the date, contents, extent and arrangement of the *Garland*, see the Introduction to *Hellenistic Epigrams*, ed. A.S.F. Gow and D.L. Page, vol. 1.

[6]For a brief general survey of the development of Greek epigram, see my Introduction to *The Greek Anthology* (1973), and the general works mentioned in the Select Bibliography.

The Poems of Meleager

Αἰεί μοι δύνει μὲν ἐν οὔασιν ἦχος Ἔρωτος,
ὄμμα δὲ σῖγα Πόθοις τὸ γλυκὺ δάκρυ φέρει·
οὐδ' ἡ νύξ, οὐ φέγγος ἐκοίμισεν, ἀλλ' ὑπὸ φίλτρων
ἤδη που κραδίᾳ γνωστὸς ἔνεστι τύπος.
5 ὦ πτανοί, μὴ καί ποτ' ἐφίπτασθαι μέν, Ἔρωτες,
οἴδατ' ἀποπτῆναι δ' οὐδ' ὅσον ἰσχύετε;

I

Love in silence shall
its levy of tears
draw from the eyes, ears
fill with clamour,

familiar impress
takes (already)
the heart,

darkness & light
powerless both
this charm to unwind:

Those wings, my Cupids
so strong in urging love
so weak now
at the time of separation.

Ἀχήεις τέττιξ, δροσεραῖς σταγόνεσσι μεθυσθείς
 ἀγρονόμαν μέλπεις μοῦσαν ἐρημολάλον,
ἄκρα δ' ἐφεζόμενος πετάλοις πριονώδεσι κώλοις
 αἰθίοπι κλάζεις χρωτὶ μέλισμα λύρας·
ἀλλά, φίλος, φθέγγου τι νέον δενδρώδεσι Νύμφαις
 παίγνιον, ἀντῳδὸν Πανὶ κρέκων κέλαδον,
ὄφρα φυγὼν τὸν Ἔρωτα μεσημβρινὸν ὕπνον ἀγρεύσω
 ἐνθάδ' ὑπὸ σκιερᾷ κεκλιμένος πλατάνῳ.

Ἄνθεμά σοι Μελέαγρος ἑὸν συμπαίστορα λύχνον,
 Κύπρι φίλη, μύστην σῶν θέτο παννυχίδων.

2

Cicala stoned with dew,
making your loud meadow-music
                              alone
hidden somewhere
                among high leaves
the sunburnt skeleton,
                its thin serrated
legs, scratching
            a lyre's melody!
– Sing something fresh
for the tree-nymphs
              maelid & *heliad*
a *responsus* for Pan in the meadows
& something for me
                fugitive from Love
that Meleager may take his siesta at noon here
blissfully, in the plane-tree's shade.

3

Witness of Cyprian nights
this lamp accept, O Cypris:
votive from Thy votary.

Ναὶ τὰν Κύπριν, Ἔρως, φλέξω τὰ σὰ πάντα πυρώσας
  τόξα τε καὶ Σκυθικὴν ἰοδόκον φαρέτρην.
φλέξω ναί· τί μάταια γελᾷς καὶ σιμὰ σεσηρὼς
  μυχθίζεις; τάχα που Σαρδάνιον γελάσεις.
ἦ γάρ σευ τὰ ποδηγὰ Πόθων ὠκύπτερα κόψας
  χαλκόδετον σφίγξω σοῖς περὶ ποσσὶ πέδην.
καίτοι Καδμεῖον κράτος οἴσομεν εἴ σε πάροικον
  ψυχῇ συζεύξω, λύγκα παρ' αἰπολίοις.
ἀλλ' ἴθι, δυσνίκητε, λαβὼν δ' ἔπι κοῦφα πέδιλα
  ἐκπέτασον ταχινὰς εἰς ἑτέρους πτέρυγας.

4

By Cypris, Cupid!
I'll burn the Bow!
burn the Arrows!
burn that fancy
Scythian Quiver!
burn, Cupid, burn
Love's bitter
armoury.
    You titter?
Why? You wrinkle up
your silly nose?
You'll titter when
I've clipped those wings
turned lust to lead
 & bound brass bands
about your feet.
But chained too near
where my Heart lies,
that were indeed
to set the lynx
to watch the fold–
best did I not
seek to best you:
take instead these
feathered shoes, on them
 & those incal-
culable wings
go! – plague elsewhere
some other (yet
ingenuous
devotee of
Fairest Cypris.

Τὴν περινηχομένην ψυχὴν ἂν πολλάκι καίῃς,
φεύξετ', Ἔρως· καὐτή, σχέτλι', ἔχει πτέρυγας.

Ματρὸς ἔτ' ἐν κόλποισιν ὁ νήπιος ὀρθρινὰ παίζων
ἀστραγάλοις τοὐμὸν πνεῦμ' ἐκύβευσεν Ἔρως.

5

Burn not too oft who flutters at thy flame
Cupid:
    Psyche, like thee, has wings.

6

Cupid at Venus' breast
    with Venus' dice
        gambols at dawn:

Gambols? Gambles!
    The stakes each morning –
        Meleager's heart.

Ἤν τι πάθω, Κλεόβουλε, — τὸ γὰρ πλέον ἐν πυρὶ παίδων
   βαλλόμενος κεῖμαι, — λείψανον ἐν σποδιῇ,
λίσσομαι, ἀκρήτῳ μέθυσον πρὶν ὑπὸ χθόνα θέσθαι,
   κάλπιν ἐπιγράψας, 'δῶρον Ἔρως Ἀίδῃ'.

Ἡδύ τί μοι διὰ νυκτὸς ἐνύπνιον ἁβρὰ γελῶντος
   ὀκτωκαιδεκέτους παιδὸς ἔτ' ἐν χλαμύδι
ἤγαγ' Ἔρως ὑπὸ χλαῖναν· ἐγὼ δ' ἁπαλῷ περὶ χρωτὶ
   στέρνα βαλὼν κενεὰς ἐλπίδας ἐδρεπόμην.
καί μ' ἔτι νῦν θάλπει μνήμης πόθος, ὄμμασι δ' ὕπνον
   ἀγρευτὴν πτηνοῦ φάσματος αἰὲν ἔχω.
ὦ δύσερως ψυχή, παῦσαί ποτε καὶ δι' ὀνείρων
   εἰδώλοις κάλλευς κωφὰ χλιαινομένη.

7

When, Cleobulus, your Meleager
already half burnt out with love
shall come to his grave's edge,
let Death's urn Love's amphora be:
wine-sprinkled, the words inscribed –
'From Eros, these, to Aides, with love!'

8

Cupid one night procured for me
between my sheets an 18-year-old
boy, who laughed invitingly,
full still of boyish ways.
I, pressing close limbs to his,
breast thrust on breast,
found nothing there:
                      it was a dream.

Still that image burns before my eyes.
Still in dream these limbs those limbs attempt.

Cease, Meleager, so to consume yourself
with images of unavailing beauty.

Ὀρθροβόας δυσέρωτι κακάγγελε, νῦν, τρισάλαστε,
 ἐννύχιος κράζεις πλευροτυπῆ κέλαδον
γαῦρος ὑπὲρ κοίτας, ὅτε μοι βραχὺ τοῦτ' ἔτι νυκτός
 παιδοφιλεῖν, ἐπ' ἐμαῖς δ' ἁδὺ γελᾷς ὀδύναις;
ἅδε φίλα θρεπτῆρι χάρις; ναὶ τὸν βαθὺν ὄρθρον,
 ἔσχατα γηρύσει ταῦτα τὰ πικρὰ μέλη.

Ἡδὺς ὁ παῖς, καὶ τοὔνομ' ἐμοὶ γλυκύς ἐστι Μυΐσκος
 καὶ χαρίεις· τίν' ἔχω μὴ οὐχὶ φιλεῖν πρόφασιν;
καλὸς γάρ, ναὶ Κύπριν, ὅλος καλός· εἰ δ' ἀνιηρός,
 οἶδε τὸ πικρὸν Ἔρως συγκεράσαι μέλιτι.

9

Dawn's cock! Your namesake here
as Love's last hours slip by,
has less for you. Thrice cursed!
Three times clapping your arrogant wings
you mock an already difficult vigil.
This hand raised you, this
by dawn's first light shall snap
forever that discordant note.

10

All that he is . . . does . . . is attractive
      even his name: Myiscus
         & love goes

where he goes in him
      as in Cypris beauty
         itself fulfils itself

& Cypris gives birth to Eros.
      Not affect but effect of love.
         Rue spills from the comb.

Ἁβρούς, ναὶ τὸν Ἔρωτα, τρέφει Τύρος· ἀλλὰ Μυΐσκος
ἔσβεσεν ἐκλάμψας ἀστέρας ἠέλιος.

Ἓν καλὸν οἶδα τὸ πᾶν, ἓν μοι μόνον οἶδε τὸ λίχνον
ὄμμα, Μυΐσκον ὁρᾶν· τἄλλα δὲ τυφλὸς ἐγώ.
πάντα δ' ἐκεῖνον ἐμοὶ φαντάζεται· ἆρ' ἐσορῶσιν
ὀφθαλμοὶ ψυχῇ πρὸς χάριν οἱ κόλακες;

11

The regions of Tyre are noted
    for the delicate beauty of their people.

And do not the bright regions of the sky
    pale when Myiscus steps forth?

12

Eyes,
    flatterers of Soul
looking on naught
    save that which soul desires,
as mine,
    blind to all else
save that alone which Myiscus can yield.

Ἐν σοὶ τἀμά, Μυΐσκε, βίου πρυμνήσι' ἀνῆπται,
ἐν σοὶ καὶ ψυχῆς πνεῦμα τὸ λειφθὲν ἔτι.
ναὶ γὰρ δὴ τὰ σά, κοῦρε, τὰ καὶ κωφοῖσι λαλεῦντα
ὄμματα, ναὶ μὰ τὸ σὸν φαιδρὸν ἐπισκύνιον,
ἤν μοι συννεφὲς ὄμμα βάλῃς ποτὲ χεῖμα δέδορκα,
ἢν δ' ἱλαρὸν βλέψῃς ἡδὺ τέθηλεν ἔαρ.

Ἠγρεύθην ⟨ὁ⟩ πρόσθεν ἐγώ ποτε τοῖς δυσέρωσι
κώμοις ἠιθέων πολλάκις ἐγγελάσας·
καί μ' ἐπὶ σοῖς ὁ πτανὸς Ἔρως προθύροισι, Μυΐσκε,
στῆσεν ἐπιγράψας, 'σκῦλ' ἀπὸ Σωφροσύνης'.

13

The breath of my life – no less,
    this rope that constrains
me, Myiscus, to you
    – you have me fast.

Sweet boy,
    even a deaf-mute
could *hear* what you *look*!
    Look blackly at me,
winter breaks out in clouds.
    Smile with clear eyes,
& spring giggles
    coating me with petals.

14

And now I, Meleager, am among them,
    those whom I mocked,
the young men crying through the evening
    to their señoritas.
For Cupid has nailed me to your gates,
    Myiscus,
on my brow cut mocking words:
    'Lo! The Fruit of Favours long Preserved.'

Εἰνόδιον στείχοντα μεσημβρινὸν εἶδον Ἄλεξιν
 ἄρτι κόμαν καρπῶν κειρομένου θέρεος·
διπλαῖ δ' ἀκτῖνές με κατέφλεγον, αἱ μὲν Ἔρωτος
 παιδὸς ἀπ' ὀφθαλμῶν, αἱ δὲ παρ' ἠελίου.
ἀλλ' ἃς μὲν νὺξ αὖθις ἐκοίμισεν, ἃς δ' ἐν ὀνείροις
 εἴδωλον μορφῆς μᾶλλον ἀνεφλόγισεν·
λυσίπονος δ' ἑτέροις ἐπ' ἐμοὶ πόνον ὕπνος ἔτευξεν
 ἔμπνουν πῦρ ψυχῇ κάλλος ἀπεικονίσας.

Ἡδὺ μὲν ἀκρήτῳ κεράσαι γλυκὺ νᾶμα μελισσῶν,
 ἡδὺ δὲ παιδοφιλεῖν καὐτὸν ἐόντα καλόν·
οἷα τὸν ἁβροκόμην στέργει Κλεόβουλον Ἄλεξις·
 †θνατὸν ὄντως τό† Κύπριδος οἰνόμελι.

15

At 12 o'clock in the afternoon
        in the middle of the street –
                Alexis.

Summer had all but brought the fruit
        to its perilous end:
                & the summer sun & that boy's look

did their work on me.
        Night hid the sun.
                Your face consumes my dreams.

Others feel sleep as feathered rest;
        mine but in flame refigures
                your image lit in me.

16

As honey in wine/ wine, honey
        Alexis in Cleobulus
Cleobulus in Alexis
        sweet-haired & lovely each
as he with whom the other
        mingles . . . product
of such two entwined
        potent
as vineyards of deathless Cypris.

Διψῶν ὡς ἐφίλησα θέρευς ἁπαλόχροα παῖδα
  εἶπα τότ' αὐχμηρὰν δίψαν ἀποπροφυγών,
'Ζεῦ πάτερ, ἆρα φίλημα τὸ νεκτάρεον Γανυμήδευς
  πίνεις, καὶ τόδε σοι χείλεσιν οἰνοχοεῖ;
καὶ γὰρ ἐγὼ τὸν καλὸν ἐν ἠιθέοισι φιλήσας
  'Αντίοχον ψυχῆς ἡδὺ πέπωκα μέλι'.

I was thirsty.
It was hot.
I kissed the boy
with girl-soft skin.
My thirst was quenched.
I said: Is that what
upstairs you're up
to Papa Zeus,
is that what strip-
ling Ganymede
at table serves,
under Hera's
watchful eye?

Lip-spilt wine
from soul to soul
as honeyed-sweet
as these vast draughts
Antiochus
pours now for me!

Ἢν ἐσίδω Θήρωνα, τὰ πάνθ' ὁρῶ· ἢν δὲ τὰ πάντα
βλέψω, τόνδε δὲ μή, τἄμπαλιν οὐδὲν ὁρῶ.

Οὐκέτι μοι Θήρων γράφεται καλός, οὐδ' ὁ πυραυγής
πρίν ποτε, νῦν δ' ἤδη δαλὸς Ἀπολλόδοτος.
στέργω θῆλυν ἔρωτα· δασυτρώγλων δὲ πίεσμα
λασταύρων μελέτω ποιμέσιν αἰγοβάταις.

18

All I see I
see in Theron.

All I see
lacking him
– nothing.

19

It is true that I held Thero fair,
    Apollodatus a torch of love –
not so no longer:
    that light is out.
Mine now woman's love.
    The delights of hirsute sex
    let us leave to Welsh shepherds.

Βεβλήσθω κύβος· ἅπτε· πορεύσομαι. — Ἠνίδε τόλμαν·
οἰνοβαρές, τίν' ἔχεις φροντίδα; — Κωμάσομαι,
κωμάσομαι. — Ποῖ, θυμέ, τρέπῃ; — Τί δ' Ἔρωτι λογισμός;
ἅπτε τάχος. — Ποῦ δ' ἡ πρόσθε λόγων μελέτη;
—Ἐρρίφθω σοφίας ὁ πολὺς πόνος· ἓν μόνον οἶδα
τοῦθ', ὅτι καὶ Ζηνὸς λῆμα καθεῖλεν Ἔρως.

HEART: My mind is made up.
   Bring the link-boy.
     I will go visit her.

HEAD: *You've been drinking all evening.*

HEART: So?
   I'll visit her drunk.
     My mind is made up.

HEAD: *Think, Meleager, think before going. Take care.*

HEART: What 'care' does Love take?
   Love leaps before looking.
    Bring the link-boy.

HEAD: *Common-sense, reason, forbid it.*

HEART: 'Reason' is nothing.
   The reasons of Zeus are as nothing.
     Under Cupid's UNREASON.

Ναὶ μὰ τὸν εὐπλόκαμον Τιμοῦς φιλέρωτα κίκιννον,
  ναὶ μυρόπνουν Δημοῦς χρῶτα τὸν ὑπναπάτην,
ναὶ πάλιν Ἰλιάδος φίλα παίγνια, ναὶ φιλάγρυπνον
  λύχνον ἐμῶν κώμων πόλλ' ἐπιδόντα τέλη·
βαιὸν ἔχω τό γε λειφθέν, Ἔρως, ἐπὶ χείλεσι πνεῦμα·
  εἰ δ' ἐθέλεις καὶ τοῦτ', εἰπὲ καὶ ἐκπτύσομαι.

By Timo's locks
> that keep Love captive,
by Demo's skin
> whence all sweet scents steal
(deluding sleep),
> by Ilias' skilled foreplay
& my ever-watchful lamp
> (each separate Venus-act
attentively recording),
> all but the last breath of my lips
has been spent in your service –

> You require that also?
Venus, it is yours:
> the poet's last gasp,
his latest (you may say)
> *ejaculation!*

Ὄρθρε, τί νῦν, δυσέραστε, βραδὺς περὶ κόσμον ἑλίσσῃ
 ἄλλος ἐπεὶ Δημοῦς θάλπεθ' ὑπὸ χλανίδι;
ἀλλ' ὅτε τὰν ῥαδινὰν κόλποις ἔχον, ὠκὺς ἐπέστης
 ὡς βάλλων ἐπ' ἐμοὶ φῶς ἐπιχαιρέκακον.

Νὺξ ἱερὴ καὶ λύχνε, συνίστορας οὔτινας ἄλλους
 ὅρκοις ἀλλ' ὑμέας εἱλόμεθ' ἀμφότεροι·
χὠ μὲν ἐμὲ στέρξειν, κεῖνον δ' ἐγὼ οὔποτε λείψειν
 ὠμόσαμεν· κοινὴν δ' εἴχετε μαρτυρίην.
νῦν δ' ὁ μὲν ὅρκιά φησιν ἐν ὕδατι κεῖνα φέρεσθαι,
 λύχνε, σὺ δ' ἐν κόλποις αὐτὸν ὁρᾷς ἑτέρων.

22

Inconstant Dawn, thou tak'st thy time
when others with Demo lie.
Why, when my turn comes,
so mockingly punctual?

23

Love's night & a lamp
judged our vows:
*that she would love me ever
& I should never leave her.*
Love's night & you, lamp,
witnessed the pact.

To-day the vow runs:
'Oaths such as these, waterwords'.
To-night, lamp,
witness her lying
         – in other arms.

Οἶδ' ὅτι μοι κενὸς ὅρκος, ἐπεὶ σέ γε τὴν φιλάσωτον
    μηνύει μυρόπνους ἀρτιβρεχὴς πλόκαμος,
μηνύει δ' ἄγρυπνον, ἰδού, βεβαρημένον ὄμμα
    καὶ σφιγκτὸς στεφάνων ἀμφὶ κόμαισι μίτος·
ἔσκυλται δ' ἀκόλαστα πεφυρμένος ἄρτι κίκιννος,
    πάντα δ' ὑπ' ἀκρήτου γυῖα σαλευτὰ φορεῖς.
ἔρρε, γύναι πάγκοινε, καλεῖ σε γὰρ ἡ φιλόκωμος
    πηκτὶς καὶ κροτάλων χειροτυπὴς πάταγος.

Foresworn now the love-vows!
    And your proclivities
Zenophile
    clamour from your appearance:
those ringlets, dripping
    with fresh application of seductive scents,
those eyes,
    heavy with sleepless nights,
and *what* is that flower doing
    dangling behind your ear?
and your hair, matted
    tousled in who knows what love-tussles –
besides which, you're *smashed*!

Go! The guitar thrums.
The castanets clatter.
Go! Woman common to all.

Ἄστρα καὶ ἡ φιλέρωσι καλὸν φαίνουσα Σελήνη
  καὶ Νὺξ καὶ κώμων σύμπλανον ὀργάνιον,
ἆρά γε τὴν φιλάσωτον ἔτ' ἐν κοίταισιν ἀθρήσω
  ἄγρυπνον λύχνῳ πόλλ' †ἀποδαομένην†·
ἤ τιν' ἔχει σύγκοιτον; ἐπὶ προθύροισι μαρανθεὶς
  δάκρυσιν ἐκδήσω τοὺς ἱκέτας στεφάνους
ἓν τόδ' ἐπιγράψας, 'Κύπρι, σοὶ Μελέαγρος ὁ μύστης
  σῶν κώμων στοργᾶς σκῦλα τάδ' ἐκρέμασε'.

Ἠοῦς ἄγγελε χαῖρε Φαεσφόρε, καὶ ταχὺς ἔλθοις
  Ἕσπερος, ἣν ἀπάγεις λάθριος αὖθις ἄγων.

25

Stars, Moon, & the Night
Love's lamps & Love's familiar
 & you my friendly Lute
that accompanies my *serenas*,

Shall we find her awake, alone,
lamenting Meleager's love
to her lamp? or wantonly
asleep beside some alien bedfellow?

Let then these tear-scalded petals
garland her door, & a note that says:
'*Cypris from Meleager*
'*graduate of the inmost ways of Love*
'*these trophies of the latest love endured*'.

26

Hail Dawn's link-boy
Lucifer/
      as Vesper
hasten
    returning
whose lovemeats
reft last night!

Ἄγγειλον τάδε, Δορκάς· ἰδοὺ πάλι δεύτερον αὐτῇ
  καὶ τρίτον ἄγγειλον, Δορκάς, ἅπαντα· τρέχε·
μηκέτι μέλλε· πέτου· βραχύ μοι βραχύ, Δορκάς, ἐπίσχες·
  Δορκάς, ποῖ σπεύδεις πρίν σε τὰ πάντα μαθεῖν;
πρόσθες δ' οἷς εἴρηκα πάλαι — μᾶλλον δέ — τί ληρῶ;
  μηδὲν ὅλως εἴπῃς· ἀλλ' ὅτι — πάντα λέγε·
μὴ φείδου †τὰ πάντα λέγε†· καίτοι τί σε, Δορκάς,
  ἐκπέμπω, σύν σοι καὐτὸς ἰδοὺ προάγων;

Εἰπὲ Λυκαινίδι, Δορκάς, 'ἴδ' ὡς ἐπίτηκτα φιλοῦσα
  ἥλως· οὐ κρύπτει πλαστὸν ἔρωτα χρόνος'.

27

Dorcas, be off! & tell her this,
tell her not once or twice but thrice –
don't loiter here! be off! – but wait,
you don't know what the message is!

Say what you said the other day
& add – at least – not *that*, but say
– say *every thing:* keep nothing back!
Tell her it all – but, no! not *you:*

Meleager has gone on before
& knocks already at her door.

28

Sweetly hath Dorcas of Lycaenis learnt:
'Kisses like coins prove true or false with time'.

Κῦμα τὸ πικρὸν Ἔρωτος ἀκοίμητοί τε πνέοντες
ζῆλοι καὶ κώμων χειμέριον πέλαγος,
ποῖ φέρομαι; πάντῃ δὲ φρενῶν οἴακες ἀφεῖνται·
ἦ πάλι τὴν τρυφερὴν Σκύλλαν ἐποψόμεθα;

Ἁ φίλερως χαροποῖς Ἀσκληπιὰς οἷα Γαλήνης
ὄμμασι συμπείθει πάντας ἐρωτοπλοεῖν.

29

Love (they say) has salt waves
jealousy, winds forbidding sleep
 & all our parties end in winter seas.

Whence & whither, Meleager?
whose wits, lacking a helmsman,
seem totally boxed . . .

There was a Barbie Doll called 'Scylla':
will she come to me again?

30

Asclepias who loves to love
invites with summer-seeming eyes
to sail upon her inland seas.

Ἰξὸν ἔχεις τὸ φίλημα, τὰ δ' ὄμματα, Τιμάριον, πῦρ·
 ἢν ἐσίδῃς καίεις, ἢν δὲ θίγῃς δέδεκας.

Ὁ τρυφερὸς Διόδωρος ἐς ἠιθέους φλόγα βάλλων
 ἤγρευται λαμυροῖς ὄμμασι Τιμαρίου,
τὸ γλυκύπικρον Ἔρωτος ἔχων βέλος. ἦ τόδε καινόν
 θάμβος ὁρῶ· φλέγεται πῦρ πυρὶ καιόμενον.

31

'Tis Timarion,
my Desire,
whose kisses sting
whose looks burn
– lips of honey
eyes of fire!

32

Diodorus, our flame of seduction,
is himself hooked
on Timarion's bright look:
stung by Cupid's rue,
not eased by Cupid's honey.
A phenomenon –
              Flame on flame with flame!

Τὸν ταχύπουν ἔτι παῖδα συναρπασθέντα τεκούσης
    ἄρτι μ' ἀπὸ στέρνων οὐατόεντα λαγών
ἐν κόλποις στέργουσα διέτρεφεν ἡ γλυκερόχρως
    Φανίον εἰαρινοῖς ἄνθεσι βοσκόμενον.
οὐδέ με μητρὸς ἔτ' εἶχε πόθος, θνήσκω δ' ὑπὸ θοίνης
    ἀπλήστου πολλῇ δαιτὶ παχυνόμενος·
καί μου πρὸς κλισίᾳ κρύψεν νέκυν, ὡς ἐν ὀνείροις
    αἰὲν ὁρᾶν κοίτης γειτονέοντα τάφον.

33

Orphaned to pleasure
    Phanion
of exquisite complexion,
    petal-pampered
fleet-footed
    with towering ears
I was reared in her soft lap
    & loved there.
When my Mother died
    what was that to me?
My life passed
    in seductive feasts
of spring flowers.
    I put on weight.
And died.
    My grave her bedside is,
that sweet Phanion
    in her sweet dreams
may know me close at hand.

Ἁδὺ μέλος, ναὶ Πᾶνα τὸν Ἀρκάδα, πηκτίδι μέλπεις,
Ζηνοφίλα, ναὶ Πᾶν', ἁδὺ κρέκεις τι μέλος.
ποῖ σε φύγω; πάντη με περιστείχουσιν Ἔρωτες,
οὐδ' ὅσον ἀμπνεῦσαι βαιὸν ἐῶσι χρόνον.
ἢ γάρ μοι μορφὰ βάλλει πόθον ἢ πάλι μοῦσα
ἢ χάρις ἢ – τί λέγω; πάντα· πυρὶ φλέγομαι.

Sweet, by Arcadian Pan
    the music that you make
Zenophile/ sweet
    (by Pan)
the Lydian lyre
    when you strike it.
Where shall I go?
    With Cupids fluttering
about me/ the air
    stifled with longing.
What words shall I speak?
    Who looks only for your beauty
who looks for your song
    for your body moving,
where all things flame
    I, who burn.

Ἡδυμελεῖς Μοῦσαι σὺν πηκτίδι καὶ Λόγος ἔμφρων
σὺν πειθοῖ καὶ Ἔρως †καλὸς ἐφ' ἡνιόχῳ†
Ζηνοφίλα, σοὶ σκῆπτρα Πόθων ἀπένειμαν, ἐπεί σοι
αἱ τρισσαὶ Χάριτες τρεῖς ἔδοσαν χάριτας.

Are not the Graces
with their Gifts
well met in thee
Zenophile?

Who knows well to:
pick out a tune on the piano
articulate in seductive accents
 & always make the most of herself:

Cupid's Love's,
the Heart's empery
under one
pink thumb.

Ἤδη λευκόιον θάλλει, θάλλει δὲ φίλομβρος
νάρκισσος, θάλλει δ' οὐρεσίφοιτα κρίνα·
ἤδη δ' ἡ φιλέραστος, ἐν ἄνθεσιν ὥριμον ἄνθος,
Ζηνοφίλα Πειθοῦς ἡδὺ τέθηλε ῥόδον.
λειμῶνες, τί μάταια κόμαις ἔπι φαιδρὰ γελᾶτε;
ἁ γὰρ παῖς κρέσσων ἁδυπνόων στεφάνων.

Τίς μοι Ζηνοφίλαν λαλιὰν παρέδειξεν ἑταίραν;
τίς μίαν ἐκ τρισσῶν ἤγαγέ μοι Χάριτα;
ἦ ῥ' ἐτύμως ἀνὴρ κεχαρισμένον ἄνυσεν ἔργον
δῶρα διδοὺς καὐτὰν τὰν Χάριν ἐν χάριτι.

36

White violets flower
lilies on hill-slopes
narcissus nodding to rain-showers

and the queen of lovers' hopes
the sweet persuasive rose,
Zenophile, more fair than those:

O hills O fields your laughter rings
falsely through the flowered spring
for she outshines your garlanding.

37

Grazie, whatever Fate gratuitously
fingered my Zenophile for me,
who talks (gift of the three Graces)
while she loves: thus is her own grace
doubled. *Grazie, grazie,* indeed.

Πταίης μοι κώνωψ ταχὺς ἄγγελος, οὔασι δ' ἄκροις
   Ζηνοφίλας ψαύσας προσψιθύριζε τάδε·
'ἄγρυπνος μίμνει σε, σὺ δ' ὦ λήθαργε φιλούντων
   εὕδεις'. εἶα πέτευ, ναὶ φιλόμουσε πέτευ·
ἥσυχα δὲ φθέγξαι, μὴ καὶ σύγκοιτον ἐγείρας
   κινήσῃς ἐπ' ἐμοὶ ζηλοτύπους ὀδύνας.
ἢν δ' ἀγάγῃς τὴν παῖδα, δορᾷ στέψω σε λέοντος,
   κώνωψ, καὶ δώσω χειρὶ φέρειν ῥόπαλον.

Volatile mosquito,
at her ear a-
buzz with love-bites
hum these words:
> 'One wakeful waits.
> 'Thou heedless sleep'st.
> 'Love slips away'.

Hence, impish Muse!
Mosquito, hence!
Ma pian' piano
with your buzzing
lest thou sting an
husband me-ward,
rancorously bent.

Bring me my girl.
This Herculean
chore perform &
thou shalt have from
grateful Meleager
fitting accoutrements
withal:
> One hero's club to swing!
> One lion pelt to wear!

Τὸ σκύφος ἡδὺ γέγηθε, λέγει δ' ὅτι τᾶς φιλέρωτος
 Ζηνοφίλας ψαύει τοῦ λαλιοῦ στόματος·
ὄλβιον· εἴθ' ὑπ' ἐμοῖς νῦν χείλεσι χείλεα θεῖσα
 ἀπνευστὶ ψυχὰν τὰν ἐν ἐμοὶ προπίοι.

Counts itself lucky
      the wine-cup!
Lip slipt
      'twixt thy lips
pouring
      sweet gossip
Zenophile.

Lucky the cup,
      more fortunate
still, Meleager
      my lip to thy lip
inclining/ you
      with a swig at my love
downed,
      like a flask of retsina!

Εὕδεις, Ζηνοφίλα, τρυφερὸν θάλος· εἴθ' ἐπὶ σοὶ νῦν
ἄπτερος εἰσῄειν ὕπνος ἐπὶ βλεφάροις,
ὡς ἐπὶ σοὶ μηδ' οὗτος ὁ καὶ Διὸς ὄμματα θέλγων
φοιτήσαι, κάτεχον δ' αὐτὸς ἐγώ σε μόνος.

Were I
    like Sleep
(though lacking Sleep's wings)
    to slip
between the petals
    of this sleeping
flower/ Zenophile
    (her closed lashes),

not even the sleep-
    bearer of Zeus
himself should entry force
    against such bliss.

Κηρύσσω τὸν Ἔρωτα τὸν ἄγριον· ἄρτι γὰρ ἄρτι
 ὀρθρινὸς ἐκ κοίτας ᾤχετ' ἀποπτάμενος.
ἐστὶ δ' ὁ παῖς γλυκύδακρυς, ἀείλαλος, ὠκύς, ἀθαμβής,
 σιμὰ γελῶν, πτερόεις νῶτα, φαρετροφόρος.
πατρὸς δ' οὐκέτ' ἔχω φράζειν τίνος· οὔτε γὰρ αἰθήρ
 οὐ χθών φησι τεκεῖν τὸν θρασύν, οὐ πέλαγος·
πάντῃ γὰρ καὶ πᾶσιν ἀπέχθεται· ἀλλ' ἐσορᾶτε
 μή που νῦν ψυχαῖς ἄλλα τίθησι λίνα.
καίτοι κεῖνος, ἰδού, περὶ φωλεόν· οὔ με λέληθας,
 τοξότα, Ζηνοφίλας ὄμμασι κρυπτόμενος.

Lost! Cupid!
        One lost Cupid!
Since daybreak.
          Meleager's delectable
bed empty.
       One lost boy!
Viz & to wit:
        winged,
cheeky,
    a chatterbox,
laughs & cries at the same time,
smirks,
    distrusted by all his acquaintance,
origin unknown,
        Zeus, Gea, Poseidon,
disclaim liability,
       armed & certainly dangerous,
beware!
   But a moment –
You say you have found him?
                Where?
    Lo! with fierce bow
    who lurks below
    her lashes, shoots
    where eyen flash:
    ZENOPHILE!

Πλέξω λευκόιον, πλέξω δ' ἀπαλὴν ἅμα μύρτοις
νάρκισσον, πλέξω καὶ τὰ γελῶντα κρίνα,
πλέξω καὶ κρόκον ἡδύν, ἐπιπλέξω δ' ὑάκινθον
πορφυρέην, πλέξω καὶ φιλέραστα ῥόδα,
ὡς ἂν ἐπὶ κροτάφοις μυροβοστρύχου Ἡλιοδώρας
εὐπλόκαμον χαίτην ἀνθοβολῇ στέφανος.

Ὁ στέφανος περὶ κρατὶ μαραίνεται Ἡλιοδώρας,
αὐτὴ δ' ἐκλάμπει τοῦ στεφάνου στέφανος.

42

Wreathe violets white
myrtle & slight
narcissus wreathe
wreathe laughing lilies
crocus & hyacinth
yellow, blue
Love's friend the rose:

Heliodore's
myrrhed brows,

wreathed curls
swim in petals.

43

The petals fall from Heliodora's image
that, flower of flowers, outfaces all.

Ἔγχει καὶ πάλιν εἰπέ, πάλιν πάλιν, 'Ηλιοδώρας·
  εἰπέ, σὺν ἀκρήτῳ τὸ γλυκὺ μίσγ' ὄνομα.
καί μοι τὸν βρεχθέντα μύροις καὶ χθιζὸν ἐόντα
  μναμόσυνον κείνας ἀμφιτίθει στέφανον.
δακρύει φιλέραστον, ἰδού, ῥόδον, οὕνεκα κείναν,
  ἄλλοθι κοὺ κόλποις ἡμετέροις ἐσορᾷ.

Pour this wine
& say this
name:
    'Heliodora!'

Pour again
repeat the same
till the wine &
name are one.

Crown my forehead
with these petals
dewy with the
scent she sheds.

See! The rose droops
(friend of lovers)
grieved that on
another's breast

my Heliodore
now rests her head.

Ἅρπασται· τίς †τόσσον ἐναιχμᾶσσαι ἄγριος εἶναι†
τίς τόσος ἀντᾶραι καὶ πρὸς Ἔρωτα μάχην;
ἆπτε τάχος πεύκας· καίτοι κτύπος· Ἡλιοδώρας·
βαῖνε πάλιν στέρνων ἐντὸς ἐμῶν, κραδίη.

Ναὶ τὸν Ἔρωτα θέλω τὸ παρ' οὔασιν Ἡλιοδώρας
φθέγμα κλύειν ἢ τᾶς Λατοΐδεω κιθάρας.

45

She's gone! Call Rape! Call Robbers! Violence!
Yet Mars against Cupid makes no sense.
Torches ho! Wait: her footsteps – All is well!
Back into my chest, heart, where safe hearts dwell.

46

More than Apollo's golden lyre
Cupid (with Meleager) would prefer
Heliodora's voice in Meleager's ear.

Ἐντὸς ἐμῆς κραδίης τὴν εὔλαλον Ἡλιοδώραν
ψυχὴν τῆς ψυχῆς ἔπλασεν αὐτὸς Ἔρως.

Τρηχὺς ὄνυξ, ὑπ' Ἔρωτος ἀνέτραφες Ἡλιοδώρας·
ταύτης γὰρ δύνει κνίσμα καὶ ἐς κραδίην.

47

In heart's space hath Eros
set shaping my spirit
to her spirit, the sweet
gossip – *Heliodora!*

48

Love cast!
Love filed!
Heliodora's
finger
      nail
whose deli-
cate scratches
prick the heart.

Ἀνθοδίαιτε μέλισσα, τί μοι χροὸς Ἡλιοδώρας
ψαύεις ἐκπρολιποῦσ' εἰαρινὰς κάλυκας;
ἦ σύ γε μηνύεις ὅτι καὶ γλυκὺ καὶ †δύσοιστον†
πικρὸν ἀεὶ κραδίᾳ κέντρον Ἔρωτος ἔχει;
ναὶ δοκέω τοῦτ' εἶπας· ἰὼ φιλέραστε, παλίμπους
στεῖχε· πάλαι τὴν σὴν οἴδαμεν ἀγγελίην.

Busy with love, the bumble bee
philanders through the petal'd spring
& lights on Heliodora's skin.

And have you left the stamen-cup
to tell me Cupid's arrow stings?
that Love both pain & pleasure brings
til rueful Heart heaves up:
                    'Enough'?

Thou loved of lovers, Bee, buzz off –
what zestful petals wait your tupping!
Such news to me was never new
whose honey's long been mixt with rue.

Ψυχή μοι προλέγει φεύγειν πόθον Ἡλιοδώρας
δάκρυα καὶ ζήλους τοὺς πρὶν ἐπισταμένη.
φησὶ μέν, ἀλλὰ φυγεῖν οὔ μοι σθένος· ἡ γὰρ ἀναιδὴς
αὐτὴ καὶ προλέγει καὶ προλέγουσα φιλεῖ.

Soul counsels flight
from Heliodore's affections,
'Those pangs, those tears'.

Soul warns
         but warns
sans will to flight:

incontinent &
warning still soul
turns & loves her.

Ἒν τόδε, παμμήτειρα θεῶν, λίτομαί σε, φίλη Νύξ,
  ναὶ λίτομαι κώμων σύμπλανε πότνια Νύξ·
εἴ τις ὑπὸ χλαίνῃ βεβλημένος Ἡλιοδώρας
  θάλπεται ὑπναπάτῃ χρωτὶ χλιαινόμενος,
κοιμάσθω μὲν λύχνος, ὁ δ' ἐν κόλποισιν ἐκείνης
  ῥιπτασθεὶς κείσθω δεύτερος Ἐνδυμίων.

Mother of gods
    Night
loved of lovers,
    by pact in love
 & love's toys
    grant
whoso smugly shares this night
    Heliodora's sheets
fired
    next flesh that offers
(nightly) insomnia –
    douse his desire
let him sleep
    cold on her breast
useless
    as Endymion.

Ὠ Νύξ, ὦ φιλάγρυπνος ἐμοὶ πόθος Ἡλιοδώρας
  καὶ †σκολιῶν ὄρθρων† κνίσματα δακρυχαρῆ,
ἆρα μένει στοργῆς ἐμὰ λείψανα, καί τι φίλημα
  μνημόσυνον ψυχρᾷ θάλπετ' ἐνὶ κλισίᾳ;
ἆρά γ' ἔχει σύγκοιτα τὰ δάκρυα, κἀμὸν ὄνειρον
  ψυχαπάτην στέρνοις ἀμφιβαλοῦσα φιλεῖ;
ἢ νέος ἄλλος ἔρως, νέα παίγνια; μήποτε, λύχνε,
  ταῦτ' ἐσίδῃς, εἴης δ' ἧς παρέδωκα φύλαξ.

Night & Night's longing
cruel tears at crueller dawn,

does Heliodora show
still my love?

Can thought (that's cold)
warm to old kisses?

Does she (as I)
take tears to bed,

kiss in dream & strain
phantom to breast?

Or lies she now new love beside?

Lamp, light never that.
Votive, light her alone.

Δάκρυά σοι καὶ νέρθε διὰ χθονός, Ἡλιοδώρα,
 δωροῦμαι, στοργᾶς λείψανον εἰς Ἀίδαν,
δάκρυα δυσδάκρυτα· πολυκλαύτῳ δ' ἐπὶ τύμβῳ
 σπένδω μνᾶμα πόθων, μνᾶμα φιλοφροσύνας.
οἰκτρὰ γὰρ οἰκτρὰ φίλαν σε καὶ ἐν φθιμένοις Μελέαγρος
 αἰάζω, κενεὰν εἰς Ἀχέροντα χάριν.
αἰαῖ ποῦ τὸ ποθεινὸν ἐμοὶ θάλος; ἅρπασεν Ἀίδας,
 ἅρπασεν, ἀκμαῖον δ' ἄνθος ἔφυρε κόνις.
ἀλλά σε γουνοῦμαι, Γᾶ παντρόφε, τὰν πανόδυρτον
 ἠρέμα σοῖς κόλποις, μᾶτερ, ἐναγκαλίσαι.

Tears, reliquaries of love,
    do they reach you in Hell,
Heliodore?
    On your sad grave
I shed them,
    seals of desire
seals of our tenderness together.
    In pain, pain
the tears come.

    As though still alive
you are mine/ my gift
    wasted in Acheron/ you
as the flower half-opened.
    And Dis, Dis has bereft us
of you:
    Earth soils the blossoming petal.

Earth! Meleager craves this:
Nourish, as all things you nourish,
Her, the too-soon-reft-bud
Let her flower finally –
Heliodora! – close at your breast.

Οὐκέθ' ὁμοῦ χιμάροισιν ἔχειν βίον, οὐκέτι ναίειν
ὁ τραγόπους ὀρέων Πὰν ἐθέλω κορυφάς.
τί γλυκύ μοι, τί ποθεινὸν ἐν οὔρεσιν; ὤλετο Δάφνις,
Δάφνις ὃς ἡμετέρῃ πῦρ ἔτεκ' ἐν κραδίῃ.
ἄστυ τόδ' οἰκήσω, θηρῶν δέ τις ἄλλος ἐπ' ἄγρην
στελλέσθω· τὰ πάροιθ' οὐκέτι Πανὶ φίλα.

Goat-foot Pan has quit his flocks.
What to him the hillslopes?
What to him the herds of mountain goats?
Their upland pastures pleasure him no more.

For Daphnis is dead. Daphnis, the fire
in sly-foot Pan, is stilled.
And Pan must now through cities go.
Others shall serve the wild flocks.
Not for Pan where Daphnis haunts no more.

Οὐ γάμον ἀλλ' Ἀίδαν ἐπινυμφίδιον Κλεαρίστα
  δέξατο παρθενίας ἅμματα λυομένα.
ἄρτι γὰρ ἑσπέριοι νύμφας ἐπὶ δικλίσιν ἄχευν
  λωτοί, καὶ θαλάμων ἐπλαταγεῦντο θύραι.
ἠῷοι δ' ὀλολυγμὸν ἀνέκραγον, ἐκ δ' Ὑμέναιος
  σιγαθεὶς γοερὸν φθέγμα μεθαρμόσατο.
αἱ δ' αὐταὶ καὶ φέγγος ἐδᾳδούχουν περὶ παστῷ
  πεῦκαι καὶ φθιμένᾳ νέρθεν ἔφαινον ὁδόν.

Παμμῆτορ Γῆ, χαῖρε· σὺ τὸν πάρος οὐ βαρὺν εἰς σέ
  Αἰσιγένην καὐτὴ νῦν ἐπέχοις ἀβαρής.

Whose the hand unloosed Clearista's zone
    at bride-night, in her bride-room?
Death, in guise of the bridegroom.

Evening, & flutes & clapping hands
    clamour at bridal door.
At dawn the funeral wail. No more

the Hymen song. The very lights
    that lit the bridal bed
light now Clearista's journey to the dead.

Weigh lightly, Earth, Great Mother of us all
on one who, living, lightly trod on you.

Εὐκράτεω Μελέαγρον ἔχω, ξένε, τὸν σὺν Ἔρωτι
καὶ Μούσαις κεράσανθ' ἡδυλόγους Χάριτας.

Ἀτρέμας, ὦ ξένε, βαῖνε· παρ' εὐσεβέσιν γὰρ ὁ πρέσβυς
  εὕδει κοιμηθεὶς ὕπνον ὀφειλόμενον
Εὐκράτεω Μελέαγρος, ὁ τὸν γλυκύδακρυν Ἔρωτα
  καὶ Μούσας ἱλαραῖς συστολίσας χάρισιν·
ὃν θεόπαις ἤνδρωσε Τύρος Γαδάρων θ' ἱερὰ χθών,
  Κῶς δ' ἐρατὴ Μερόπων πρέσβυν ἐγηροτρόφει.
ἀλλ' εἰ μὲν Σύρος ἐσσί, σαλάμ· εἰ δ' οὖν σύ γε Φοῖνιξ,
  ναίδιος· εἰ δ' Ἕλλην, χαῖρε· τὸ δ' αὐτὸ φράσον.

57

You stand where Meleager lies, son of Eucrates,
in whom the honeyed Graces, Eros, & the Muses met.

58

Tread lightly, Stranger!
    Here, among the Faithful Dead
An old man lies,
    Sleeping the sleep
That all must sleep –
    Meleager, son of Eucrates,
Whose verses truly blend
    Love's sweet & sad tears,
The Muses,
    & the ribald Graces.
Tyre of Heavenly origin,
    Gadara's Holy earth,
Made him man;
    Meropian Cos
Harboured his old age.
    Be you Syrian: 'Salam!'
Phoenician: 'Audoni!'
    Greek: 'Chairè!'
And see, before you leave this place,
    You say the same to him.

Literal Translations and Notes

The cribs are intended only as a guide to the literal content of the Greek poems. Odd constructions which would be inadmissible in English prose are used freely whenever they seem the best aid to construing the Greek. As far as possible I have tried to use appropriate connotative vocabulary; and have generally repeated the same English words or phrases for recurrent Greek words, compounds and phrases.

A case worth clarifying is the rendering of *Erōs* or *erōs*. I translate *erōs* as 'love', whether on its own or in compounds. When Love personified, Aphrodite's winged archer-boy whom we know better as Cupid, is clearly intended I translate *Erōs* as 'Eros'; but 'Love' when the context is indecisive between the personification and a more general abstraction. *Erōtes* in the plural (Cupids) I translate as 'Loves'. (They are sometimes also called *Pothoi*, 'Desires'.) *erōs* denotes a specifically sexual feeling, while *philia* – though it may include this – has the more general sense of affection, fondness, etc.; its various forms are here translated as 'love' or 'like', according to context.

Notes and occasional explanatory matter appear in italic type within square brackets [ ]; supplements to fill in sense 'understood' or suppressed in the Greek are in roman type. References in parentheses at the head of the versions are to the numbering of the poems both in Gow and Page's *Hellenistic Epigrams* (roman numerals) and The Palatine Anthology.

1 (X, 5.212)

Always the noise of Love enters into [*or* sinks into – *the word is often used of the sun setting*] my ears, [my] eye in silence offers [*or* bears] this sweet tear to the Desires. Neither night nor daylight puts [it – *love* or *me?*] to sleep [*or* rest], but already the [love-] spells' well-known stamp is set on my heart. O winged Loves, is it that you know how to fly towards [us], but have no power at all to fly away?

   The first line is reminiscent of Sappho's famous poem – Lobel & Page 31, 11-12 – 'my eyes see nothing & thunder/ sounds in my ears, . . .' (tr. Peter Whigham) – though Meleager's phrasing is more closely modelled on Kallimachos AP 5.6, line 4. Jacobs' suggestion δινεῖ is, in the context of Sappho's image, very attractive – 'Always in my ears the noise of Love spins round' – but it is improbable since Kallimachos uses δύνειν.

2 (XIII, 7.196)

Noisy cricket, drunk with dew-drops, you sing your country song which fills lonely places with chatter; with saw-like legs and negro [*or* sunburnt] skin, sitting on the tips of leaves you shriek lyre-music. But dear [friend], utter some new ditty for the woodland Nymphs, strike up a tune in response to Pan, so that escaping from Eros I may snatch a midday sleep, lying here beneath a shady plane-tree.

   A blend of the pastoral, descriptive and erotic types of epigram. Peter Whigham's *maelids* are nymphs first introduced by Ezra Pound – cf. his poem based on Ibykos, 'The Spring' – embodying the spirits of the apple-tree.

3 (XI, 6.162)

To you dear Kypris Meleager dedicates this offering, the lamp his playmate, initiate of your night-festivals.

This and AP 6.163 (not included here) are Meleager's only dedicatory epigrams – though others (like poem 25) use some of the props of the genre.

4 (VII, 5.179)

Yes by Kypris, Eros, I'll burn them, set fire to all your bows and Scythian arrow-holding quiver, I'll burn them, by – why are you foolishly laughing, why sneeringly [lit. with turned-up nose] grin and snigger? You'll soon be laughing bitterly [or ruefully]. For I'll cut those swift wings of yours which guide the Desires, and tie up your feet with bronze-binding shackles. But we will have a Kadmeian ['Pyrrhic' is an almost exact equivalent] victory, if I chain you next to my soul, [like] a lynx by a goat-fold. So be off, you hard-to-defeat one; taking your light sandals, spread your quick wings towards [or against] others.

An inversion of a traditional theme – here the lover is the hunter, Eros his prey.

5 (XIV, 5.57)

Eros, if you persist in scorching the *psyche* which flutters [lit. swims] round [you], she will fly away: she too, cruel one [*Eros*], has wings.

'A highly sophisticated epigram, exquisitely expressed in a dozen words. Ψυχή signifies both *soul* and *butterfly*: Ἔρως is the flame; the lover's ψυχή flutters round it; Ἔρως is warned not to burn the ψυχή, which is itself, like Eros, winged, and will fly out of his reach if hurt.' – Gow and Page. 'Probably on a gem which represented a butterfly, the usual emblem of the soul in later classical art, fluttering round a lamp.' – Mackail.

6 (XV, 12.47)

Still in his mother's lap, the child Eros, playing with knuckle-bones in the morning, gambled my life [lit. breath (of being)] away.

7 (XCVII, 12.74)

If anything happens to me [*same euphemism in Greek*], Kleoboulos, – for I lie almost wholly [*lit.* the greater part] thrown into the fire of [love of] boys – intoxicate with unmixed wine, I pray, the remnant of me in the ashes before you lay it under the earth, and inscribe on my urn 'A gift from Eros to Hades'.

Combines the themes of the erotic and sepulchral epigram, with a touch of characteristic exaggeration in the desire to have his dead body made drunk (wine was normally consumed 'mixed' – i.e. diluted with water). Pouring wine on the ashes of the dead was a standard practice.

8 (CXVII, 12.125)

Eros brought me through the night [as I slept] under the blanket rather a pleasant dream, of an eighteen-year-old boy, delicately laughing, still wearing the *chlamys* [*short cloak worn by 'epheboi', adolescents aged 17–20*]; and pressing my chest to his soft flesh, I plucked empty hopes. And longing for the memory [*i.e. the object of the memory*] heats me still; in my eyes I continually retain the sleep which hunts the winged vision. O soul unlucky in love, stop finally being warmed vainly, even in dreams, by images of beauty.

9 (CXVIII, 12.137)

Dawn-crier, bringer of bad news [*lit.* bad-herald] to a man unlucky in love, now, thrice-accursed-one, you shriek in the night with a clashing as you beat your sides, exultant over [my] bed – when this short [bit] of night is [all that is left] for me to make love with the boy – and you mock sweetly at my pains? This [is] the loving thanks [you give] to the one who feeds you [*or* brought you up]? By the dim morning twilight [*lit.* deep dawn], you will be singing this bitter song for the last time.

Cf. poem 22.

10 (CVII, 12.154)

Pleasant the boy, and Myiskos' name [*lit.* Myiskos in respect of his name] is sweet to me and charming. What excuse have I not to love him? He's beautiful, by Kypris, entirely beautiful; and if troublesome, [well –] Eros knows how to [*i.e. is accustomed to*] mix bitterness with honey.

Based on Asklepiades' poem, AP 12.153.

11 (C, 12.59)

Týre brings up delicate [*or* graceful] boys, by Eros. But Myiskos, flaring out, a sun, extinguishes the stars.

The compliment, though different in other respects, has in common with poem 43 on Heliodora the use of the verb *eklampein* ('to flare out' or 'shine out').

12 (CIV, 12.106)

I know one wholly beautiful thing, my gluttonous eye knows one thing alone – to look at Myiskos; for everything else I am blind. Everything conjures up his image [*the usage of* phantazesthai *is unparalleled*] for me. Do the eyes look on [only] what pleases the soul, – the flatterers?

13 (CVIII, 12.159)

On you, Myiskos, my life's [stern-]cables are fastened; on you [depends] the breath [of being] still left to my soul. Yes by your eyes, boy, which talk even to the deaf, and by your beaming eyebrows – if you should ever cast a clouded glance [*lit.* eye] at me, I stare at winter; if you look happily, sweet spring is in bloom.

14 (XCIX, 12.23)

I am trapped, who once in the past often laughed mockingly at the serenades of young bachelors unhappily in love. And at your doors, Myiskos, winged Eros has fixed me, inscribing – 'Spoils [won] from Temperance'.

Compare poem 25. The word *kōmos* is here, and in poems 20, 21, 24, 25, 29 and 51, loosely translated as 'serenade'. For its implications see the 'Note on Garlands, Symposia and the Kōmos'.

15 (LXXIX, 12.127)

I saw Alexis walking on the road at midday, when the summer was just being shorn of its fruit's tresses. Double rays burned me: those of Love from the boy's eyes, and those from the sun. Night put these [latter] to rest: but a phantom of [his] beauty increasingly kindled the others in my dreams. Sleep, for others the releaser-from-pain [*or* toil], brought pain to me – imaging in my soul a beauty, a living fire.

The setting of the encounter is slightly reminiscent of Rhianos (AP 12.121); the poem is otherwise quite fresh. One of Baron Corvo's more lyrical notes to his translation extols the poem's subtleties of alliteration, assonance, cadence and the rhythmical shift from the dactylic hexameter to the predominantly spondaic pentameter of the last couplet.

16 (LXXX, 12.164)

It is pleasant to mix with unmixed wine the bees' sweet fluid, pleasant to love a boy when you yourself are beautiful – just as Alexis loves soft-haired Kleoboulos. These two are the immortal mead [*lit.* honey-wine] of Kypris.

Translating Paton's ἀθάνατον τούτω in line 4. Kleoboulos is probably not the same person as the friend addressed in poem 7.

17 (LXXXIV, 12.133)

In summer, thirsty as I kissed the tender-skinned boy, when I had escaped my parching thirst, I said, 'Father Zeus, do you drink Ganymede's nectary kiss, is this the wine he pours to your lips [*or* to you with his lips]? Now that I have kissed Antiochos, the [most] beautiful among youths, I have drunk the delicious honey of the soul.'

Cf. poem 39, and Meleager's poem (AP 12.65), which reads literally – 'If Zeus still is the sort who once snatched Ganymede at his youth's peak, to have him as a cupbearer of his nectar, where shall I hide beautiful Myiskos in my heart, to prevent Zeus unawares to me swooping on the boy with his wings?' Zeus captured Ganymede by taking the form of an eagle.

18 (XCV, 12.60)

If I look at Theron, I see everything: but if I view everything, and not him, once more I see nothing.

19 (XCIV, 12.41)

Theron is no longer counted beautiful by me, nor Apollódatos, once gleaming like fire in the past, now already a smouldering brand [*i.e. nearly burnt-out torch*]. I am fond of [*or* content with] the love of women. Let the hugging of hairy-arsed passives [? – *rare word of uncertain meaning*] be the concern of goat-mounting shepherds.

Similar 'renunciations' are made by several later epigrammatists, including Strato – whose love-poems are exclusively homosexual.

20 (XIX, 12.117)

'Let the die be cast: light up: I'm on my way.' – 'Look, what boldness! Wine-loaded, what intention do you have?' 'I'll go serenading, serenading.' – 'Where are you turning to, [my] mind?' – 'What's logic-chopping [*lit.* reasoning] to Love? Light up at once.' – 'And where's your old concern for [*or* study of] logic?' – 'Away with the long labour of wisdom. This one thing alone I'm sure of, that Love [*or* Eros] brought down even the mind [*or* resolution] of Zeus.'

A dialogue between the drunk lover and his sober self. The division of 'speakers' in lines 1–2 is disputed. The poem is influenced by Mime, a genre of poetic monologue or dialogue comprising a single scene based on ideas from Comedy, but intended for recitation rather than acting.

21 (XXIII, 5.197)

Yes by Timo's fine-haired love-liking curls, by Demo's sleep-cheating perfume-breathing skin, again by Ilias' dear [love-]play, and my wakeful lamp which often spied on the rites of my serenades, I have only a little breath left on my lips, Eros; and if you want this too, tell me, and I'll cough up [*lit.* spit (it) out].

All the personal names in poems 21–33 (except obviously Diodoros in 32) are those of women. Timarion in poem 31 and 32 may be a diminutive form of Timo.

22 (XXVIII, 5.173)

Dawn unfavourable to lovers, why do you now revolve around the sky [*or* universe] slowly, while another keeps warm under Demo's blanket? But when I held the slender [girl] in my embrace [*lit.* bosom, lap], you arrived quickly, as if throwing on me a light which took pleasure in my distress ['*schadenfreudig*' expresses the compound almost exactly].

The premature dawn theme goes back as far as Sappho, and is commonplace among the epigrammatists.

23 (LXIX, 5.8)

Holy night and lamp, we both chose no other witnesses to our oaths but you. We swore – he to love me, and I never to leave him; common [to both of us] was the testimony you received. But now he declares those oaths are carried [away] on water, and you, lamp, see him in others' embraces [*lit.* bosom, lap].

Not definitely by Meleager – Planudes ascribes the poem to Philodemos. The lamp-motif is almost exclusively of heterosexual love, and the poem's speaker is therefore a woman. Philodemos uses a female *persona* elsewhere, but Meleager does not. The poem blends, and extends, motifs from Kallimachos (AP 5.6) and Asklepiades (AP 5.7) – poems which immediately precede it in The Palatine Anthology; the run of poems on the same theme is doubtless a fragment of Meleager's *Garland*, unless Planudes is right (but Philodemos did not appear in the *Garland*).

24 (LXX, 5.175)

I know that [your] oath is void for me, since the recently-applied scents on your hair [*lit.* just-wetted perfume-breathing hair] betrays your wantonness, betrays your sleeplessness, look, your weighed-down eyes, and the band [*lit.* thread (*of a warp*)] of your garland tight about your hair. Your recently ruffled curls are licentiously dishevelled; under the influence of unmixed wine you drag along all your staggering limbs. Be off, woman common to all. The lyre that loves serenades calls you, and the clatter of castanets rattled by the fingers.

Meleager at his most impressively elaborate – rare words and new compounds deployed energetically.

25 (LXXIII, 5.191)

Stars, and Moon shining finely for those who like love; Night, and my *organion* [*diminutive form of some musical instrument – a kind of lyre or even flute?*], fellow-roamer of my serenades, shall I see the profligate [girl] still awake in her bed, complaining much to her lamp – or has she some new bed-partner? Wasted away by weeping, I will hang my garlands [as] suppliants at her doors, inscribing this one thing: 'Kypris, to you Meleager, initiate of your serenades, has hung up these spoils of his affection.'

A cross between the erotic and dedicatory epigram, combined here with the *kōmos*-theme. In line 4 I translate Huschke's ἀποκλαομένην, the probable emendation.

26 (LXXV, 12.114)

Herald of dawn, hail, Morning Star; and may you return quickly [in the form of] the Evening Star, secretly bringing back again her whom you take away [*i.e. the girl who leaves him at dawn, and meets him clandestinely in the evening*].

27 (LXXI, 5.182)

Take this message, Dorkas; look, tell it to her again a second time, and a third time – all [of it]. Move! Don't delay, fly – wait a minute, Dorkas, a minute. Dorkas, where are you rushing to before you know everything? Add to what I told you before – or rather – what nonsense am I talking?! – Don't say anything at all – only that – tell [her] everything. Don't be sparing – tell everything. – But why am I sending you, Dorkas, since – look – I'm going with you – leading the way!?

In the style of Mime. The corruption in line 7 admits of several possible emendations with slightly different emphases, but the general sense is clear. The would-be go-between Dorkas is probably a slave-girl belonging to Lykainis, as in poem 28.

28 (LVIII, 5.187)

Tell Lykainis, Dorkas – 'See how your kisses are proved superficial [*lit.* melted-on, *i.e. plated*]. Time does not conceal a counterfeit love.'

29 (LXIV, 5.190)

Bitter wave of Love, unsleeping jealousies which blow [*i.e. gales of jealousy*], and wintry sea of serenades, which way am I being taken? The rudders of my mind are let loose in all directions; will I ever again set eyes on my tender Skylla?

The poem is addressed to Tryphera – Meleager puns on her name ('tender'). She is a Skylla (the sea-monster of mythology) either because of the risks the lover has to run in their affair, or because she is grasping (I paraphrase Jacobs' note). Tryphera appears in another poem (LXIII, 5.154) not included here.

30 (XXV, 5.156)

Love-liking Asklepias with her sparkling eyes as of [a sea's] calm, persuades all men to make the voyage of love.

31 (LIX, 5.96)

Your kiss is birdlime, your eyes, Timarion, fire. If you look at me, you burn [me]; if you touch me, you've caught [me].

32 (LXI, 12.109)

Diodoros the delieate [*or* tender, effeminate], casting [glances of] fire at the young bachelors, has been caught by the wanton [*lit.* hungry] eyes of Timarion; he carries [stuck in him] the sweet-bitter arrow of Eros. This is indeed a new wonder I see – fire ablaze, being burnt by fire.

A new twist to the old role-reversal theme – the object of homosexual attention himself the victim of love. This time, for a woman.

33 (LXV, 7.207)

Sweet-skinned Phanion loved me and brought me up in her lap, feeding me on spring flowers – a swift-footed, long-eared hare, snatched while still a baby from my mother's breast. I did not pine for my mother any more, but I died from a surfeit of feasts, grown fat from excessive banquet. She buried my corpse near her bed, so as always to see in her dreams my grave bordering on her bedstead.

The epitaph is mock-heroic, as becomes apparent by lines 5–6. This makes an interesting comparison with Catullus' subtly ironical poem (no. 3) on the death of Lesbia's pet sparrow, which has similar if less broad touches of the mock-heroic.

34 (XXIX, 5.139)

Pleasant is the tune, by Pan of Arkadia, which you play on your lyre, Zenóphila, by Pan, pleasant is the tune you play. Where shall I [go to] escape you? The Loves surround me on all sides, and they do not allow me [even] a little time, so much as to breathe. Either your beauty shoots longing into me, or again your music or grace or – what shall I say? [Your] everything. I am burning with fire.

35 (XXX, 5.140)

The melodious Muses with their lyre, Persuasion with intelligent Reason [*lit.* intelligent Reason with Persuasion], and Eros driving Beauty – [these], Zenophila, invested you with the sovereignty [*lit.* sceptres] of the Desires, since the three Graces gave you [these] three graces.

Translating in line 2 Graefe's suggestion κάλλος ὑφηνιοχῶν.

36 (XXXI, 5.144)

Already the snowdrop [?] is in bloom, and in bloom the rain-loving narcissus, and in bloom the mountain-rambling lilies; and already the amorous [*or* dear to lovers] Zenophila, spring flower among flowers, sweet rose of Persuasion, is in bloom. Meadows, why are you foolishly laughing, bright in your foliage [*lit.* tresses]? That girl is better than [any] sweet-smelling garlands.

Gow and Page find the 'mountain-rambling lilies' troublesome ('lilies do not wander and are not especially associated with hills either in fact or in literature'), and have much sympathy with Graefe's comments, which I render '... he does not usually talk with so little sobriety as to say that lilies can wander in the mountains ... a flower can never be said to be οὐρεσίφοιτος by a poet of sane mind'. Sane poets have done a lot worse. The point of Meleager's image, which does not seem very difficult, is in the appearance of flowers dotted, in straggling lines perhaps, on hillsides. They can be said to wander with no great stretch of the metaphorical imagination. John Addington Symonds, who knew the Mediterranean coasts, regarded this epithet as 'delicately true to nature' (footnote on p. 525 of *Studies of the Greek Poets*, 3rd ed., 1920).

37 (XXXII, 5.149)

Who portrayed for me Zenophila, my talkative mistress? Who brought me one of the three Graces [*lit.* one Grace of the three]? Yes, the man truly did a gracious deed – giving me a present, even the Grace herself, in his grace [*i.e. gracious gift*].

Formally, the poem is an epideictic epigram – Zenophila's portrait being the ostensible subject – merging with the love-epigram. The theme occurs in Kallimachos AP 5.146. Gow and Page point to verbal reminiscences of Erinna and Nossis, and summarize – 'a good example of the way in which M. creates a new poem by combining and adapting a variety of types and motifs and reminiscences.'

38 (XXXIV, 5.152)

Fly for me, mosquito, swift messenger, touch the tips of Zenophila's ears and whisper this – 'Insomniac he waits for you while you sleep, forgetful of those who love you.' Come, fly off – yes, musical one, fly off – but speak [to her] quietly, in case you wake her bed-partner and rouse pangs of jealousy [in him] against me. But if you bring me the girl, I'll robe you with a lion's skin, mosquito, and give you a club to carry in your hand [*i.e. I'll honour you for performing a Herculean task*].

Original in theme and treatment, and 'a good example of M.'s ironic-satirical mood' (Gow and Page). The opening is effectively onomatopoeic, with the *ps* and *sd* alliteration.

39 (XXXV, 5.171)

The glad [*or* sweet] wine-cup rejoices, and says that it touches the talkative mouth of love-liking Zenophila. Fortunate [cup]! If only she would put her lips now to *my* lips, and drink up the soul in me without drawing breath [*i.e. at one draught*].

>   Combining the motif of Plato's poem, AP 5.78 –
>
>   Kissing Agathon, I found
>   My soul at my lips. Poor thing!
>   It went there, hoping
>   To slip across.
>   [tr. Peter Jay]
>
> with that of the 'kiss in the cup' – a later example is Agathias AP 5.261:
>
>   It is not wine that makes me reel
>   Not juice of grape I crave,
>   Only to drink where you have drunk
>   A wine no grape e'er gave.

> Let but your lip the wine-cup lip
> Touch – how can I flee
> Or wine, or sweet cup-bearer, for
> The kiss it bears of thee?
> [tr. Peter Whigham]

Ben Jonson's *Song. To Celia* ('Drinke to me, onely, with thine eyes') is derived only indirectly from poems like these: his immediate source was a passage in Philostratos.

40 (XXXVI, 5.174)

You are asleep, Zenophila, tender sprig [*or in question form* – 'Are you asleep . . . ?']. If only I could come to you now, [as] Sleep [though] wingless [*Sleep himself usually being represented as winged in Greek art*] to your eyelids, so that not even he who charms the eyes of Zeus might visit you [in the future], but I would possess you [all by] myself alone.

41 (XXXVII, 5.177)

I proscribe Eros, the savage [one]! For now, just now at dawn he flew away from his bed and went. The boy is sweet-tearful, ever-talkative, quick, unabashed, sneeringly [*lit*. with turned-up nose] laughing, winged on his back, quiver-bearing. I can't go on to say whose son he is – for neither Sky nor Earth admits having given birth to the arrogant [boy], nor [does] the Sea. He is hated everywhere and by everyone. But look out, in case he may even now be laying more nets for souls. Yes [there] he [is], look, near his lair. You haven't escaped my notice, archer, by hiding yourself in Zenophila's eyes.

Blending the colloquial language of the town-crier with a theme from Moschos' poem 'The Runaway Eros' and verbal echoes of Asklepiades, Kallimachos and Antipater.

42 (XLVI, 5.147)

I will plait snowdrops, I will plait tender narcissus together with myrtle-berries, I will plait laughing lilies too, I will plait the sweet crocus; I will interweave crimson hyacinths, I will plait roses too, which are friendly to lovers – so that the garland will scatter [*lit.* flower-throw] the fine-petalled [*lit.* fine-tressed] foliage [*lit.* hair *but the metaphorical sense is common*] over the temples of Heliodora with the perfumed curls.

The last two lines are sometimes read 'so that the garland on the temples of H. with the perfumed curls, will scatter the fine locks of her hair with flowers'; but this is tautologous and misses the point of Meleager's play with the variety of words for 'hair' and the metaphorical senses. Mackail points out that flowers were scattered over people's heads as a mark of honour; Meleager's description is thus subtly allusive.

43 (XLV, 5.143)

The garland fades round Heliodora's head, but she flares out, a garland for the garland.

'It is a commonplace to say that the girl outshines the wreath; it seems much less complimentary to say that this is so at a time when the wreath is fading. The point, here so allusive as to be obscure, is explicit in Philostratos *Ep.* 9; the roses ... wither and die ... because [they] "cannot bear to be surpassed, nor could they endure the rivalry with you ..."' – Gow and Page.

44 (XLII, 5.136)

Fill up [the cup], and again say, again, again 'To Heliodora'. Say [it] and mix the sweet name with the unmixed wine [*i.e. let her name be all that is added to the wine*]. And place round [my head] the garland dripping with perfume, even though it is yesterday's, [as] a reminder of her. See how the rose, which is friendly to lovers, weeps because it sees that she is elsewhere, and not in my arms [*lit.* bosom, lap].

Variation on a theme of Kallimachos (AP 12.51) and another of Asklepiades (AP 5.145); as always in Meleager, the combination is given a new twist.

45 (LV, 12.147)

They've snatched [her]! Who is so savage as to do such violence? Who so strong [as] to raise battle against Eros himself? Quick, light the [pine-]torches. – But a footstep: Heliodora's. Get back again inside my chest, heart.

Translating in line 1 the reading of most editors, τίς τόσσον ἂν αἰχμάσαι ἄγριος εἴη. 'What we need, but cannot extract from the tradition, is τίς τόσσος ἐναιχμάσαι Ἀφρογενείῃ, "who so strong as to fight against Aphrodite?" ' – Gow and Page.

Abduction was apparently quite a possible, if infrequent, outcome of a *kōmos* – see the 'Note on Garlands, Symposia and the Kōmos'.

46 (XLIV, 5.141)

By Eros, I would rather hear Heliodora's utterance close to my ears, than the lyre of the son of Leto [*i.e. Apollo*].

47 (XLVIII, 5.155)

Within my heart Eros himself has moulded sweet-talking Heliodora, soul of my soul.

48 (XLIX, 5.157)

Heliodora's fingernail was made sharp by Eros – for her [love-]scratches penetrate even to the heart.

49 (L, 5.163)

Flower-fed bee, why do you touch my Heliodora's skin, abandoning the buds of spring? Are you demonstrating that she has a sting of Love both sweet and unendurably bitter always to the heart [*i.e. to all lovers' hearts*]? Yes, I think so – that's what you're saying. Off, friend to lovers, go on your way back; I knew your news long ago.

Translating in line 3 Salmasius' emendation δυσύποιστον, and taking it adverbially.

50 (XLI, 5.24)

My soul forewarns me to escape from desire for Heliodora, knowing well the tears and jealousies of the past. It speaks [*or* commands] – but I have not the strength to escape; for shameless she [*the soul*] both forewarns me, and while forewarning, loves [*i.e. continues to be in love with H.*].

The Palatine Anthology mss. ascribe this poem to Philodemos, though the name 'Heliodora' only occurs elsewhere in love-epigrams in Meleager's work. Neither style nor context in the Anthology resolve the uncertainty, and it is possible that the poem is an imitation of Meleager by Philodemos.

51 (LI, 5.165)

This one thing, mother of all the gods, I beseech of you, dear Night, yes beseech, holy Night, fellow-roamer of my serenades – if someone lies sprawled keeping cosy under Heliodora's blanket, warmed by her sleep-cheating skin; – let the lamp fall asleep, and let him, flattened in her embrace [*lit.* bosom, lap], lie there, a second Endymion.

Lovers keep the lamp alight; Endymion was a handsome youth loved by the Moon but doomed to perpetual sleep. The poem combines themes from two poems by Asklepiades – AP 5.7 for the lamp, AP 5.164 for the address to Night – with the Endymion motif.

52 (LII, 5.166)

O night, O insomniac longing in me for Heliodora, O gloomy dawns' torments delighting in tears, are there any relics left of her affection for me, does any kiss stay warm [as] a reminder [of me] in the cold bed? Does she have tears for bed-partners, does she hug [*lit.* clasp round] to her breasts and kiss the soul-cheating dream of me [*almost* = *ghost of me* – *Gow and Page*]? Or is there some new love, new darling [or plaything]? Never, lamp, may you look on this, but guard her whom I entrusted to you.

Translating Reiske's suggestion σκοτίων ὄρθρων in line 2. The mss. reading as obelized means 'unjust' – Mackail suggests 'jealous' or 'malign'. In line 8 I translate the received text, but as Gow and Page note, 'much better sense would be given by ὧν παρέδωκα, "be watchman over that which I have entrusted to you", viz. my own amours, not those of others.' The lamp cannot act as her guardian, since it is only alight and operative *while* she is making love with the poet or his rival.

53 (LVI, 7.476)

Tears I give to you, even down through the earth to Hades, the remnant of my love, Heliodora – tears painfully wept; and on your much-mourned tomb I pour them [as a libation], in memory of longing, in memory of affection. Piteously, piteously I Meleager lament you, dear to me even though among the dead – a useless gift to Acheron. Alas, where is my longed-for bud? Hades has snatched [her], snatched – dust dirties the flower in blossom. But I implore you, Earth who nurtures all, clasp her whom all mourn gently, mother, into your bosom.

54 (CXXVI, 7.535)

No longer do I, goat-footed Pan, want to spend my life among the goat kids, or inhabit the peaks of mountains. What is sweet to me, what desirable in the mountains? Daphnis is dead, Daphnis who gave birth to a fire in my heart. I'll make my home in this town; let someone else set out to hunt wild beasts. His former [ways] are no longer dear to Pan.

Meleager's only purely mythological epigram, doubtless based on some statue of Pan ('in this town'). Daphnis is the mythological Sicilian shepherd, of whom there are two main stories – [1] he was loved by a nymph who required total fidelity, and who blinded him after he succumbed to the combination of an amorous princess and a quantity of wine. He invented pastoral music, which he played to console himself. [2] Theokritos' version is that he was determined to love no-one; Aphrodite punished this aberration by making him fall in love. But he defied her to the end and died of unsatisfied longing; everyone, including Aphrodite, mourned him. Pan who was in love with him taught him to sing and play the pipe.

55 (CXXIII, 7.182)

Not marriage but bridal Death [*lit.* Hades] did Klearista receive, when she unloosed the girdle of her virginity. Just now in the evening the flutes [*of boxwood*] were playing at the bride's doors; and the bedroom doors were being knocked at [*a custom at wedding celebrations*]. In the morning they cried out the lament, the wedding-song [was] silenced [and] changed to an utterance of mourning. The same [pine-]torches flashed their light by the bride's bed, and lit the dead girl's downward path [*i.e. to the domain of Hades*].

A restrained poem, in which for once Meleager hardly departs from the thematic and stylistic conventions. The poem's antecedents include Kallimachos AP 7.517, Erinna AP 7.712 and Antipater of Sidon AP 7.711.

56 (CXXIV, 7.461)

Hail Earth, mother of all. May you now hold Aisigenes lightly [*lit.* unheavily], who before was not a burden [*lit.* heavy] to you.

The name 'Aisigenes' is not found elsewhere. Meleager gives a new twist to the old commonplace 'may the earth lie lightly' theme with his antithesis.

57 (7.416)

Stranger, I hold Meleager, Eukrates' son, who mixed sweet-speaking Graces with Eros and the Muses.

'Although the poem is anonymous it is surely Meleager's own response to Kallimachos' – T. B. L. Webster. The preceding poem in The Palatine Anthology, and doubtless in Meleager's original *Garland*, is Kallimachos' epitaph on himself. 'Graces' here, as in poem 58, may punningly allude to his Menippean essays.

58 (IV, 7.419)

Pass quietly, stranger. The old man sleeps among the pious [dead], lulled in the slumber which is due [for everyone]: Meleager son of Eukrates, who dressed [*or* joined] sweet-tearful Eros and the Muses with joyous graces ['*i.e. wrote good-humoured, poetical, elegant love-epigrams*' – *Gow and Page*]. Tyre of the godlike boys and Gadara's holy earth made him a man; lovely [*or* beloved] Kos of the Meropes [*traditionally the original inhabitants of the island*] looked after the old man in his age. So if you are a Syrian, Salaam! If you are a Phoenician, Naidios! If you are a Greek, Chairè! [*all three words mean 'Hail'*] – And say the same [to me].

Χείματος ἠνεμόεντος ἀπ' αἰθέρος οἰχομένοιο,
πορφυρέη μείδησε φερανθέος εἴαρος ὥρη.
γαῖα δὲ κυανέη χλοερὴν ἐστέψατο ποίην,
καὶ φυτὰ θηλήσαντα νέοις ἐκόμησε πετήλοις.
5 οἱ δ' ἁπαλὴν πίνοντες ἀεξιφύτου δρόσον Ἠοῦς
λειμῶνες γελόωσιν, ἀνοιγομένοιο ῥόδοιο.
χαίρει καὶ σύριγγι νομεὺς ἐν ὄρεσσι λιγαίνων,
καὶ πολιοῖς ἐρίφοις ἐπιτέρπεται αἰπόλος αἰγῶν.
ἤδη δὲ πλώουσιν ἐπ' εὐρέα κύματα ναῦται
10 πνοιῇ ἀπημάντῳ Ζεφύρου λίνα κολπώσαντος.
ἤδη δ' εὐάζουσι φερεσταφύλῳ Διονύσῳ,
ἄνθεϊ βοτρυόεντος ἐρεψάμενοι τρίχα κισσοῦ.
ἔργα δὲ τεχνήεντα βοηγενέεσσι μελίσσαις
καλὰ μέλει, καὶ σίμβλῳ ἐφήμεναι ἐργάζονται
15 λευκὰ πολυτρήτοιο νεόρρυτα κάλλεα κηροῦ.
πάντη δ' ὀρνίθων γενεὴ λιγύφωνον ἀείδει,
ἀλκυόνες περὶ κῦμα, χελιδόνες ἀμφὶ μέλαθρα,
κύκνος ἐπ' ὄχθαισιν ποταμοῦ, καὶ ὑπ' ἄλσος ἀηδών.
εἰ δὲ φυτῶν χαίρουσι κόμαι, καὶ γαῖα τέθηλεν,
20 συρίζει δὲ νομεύς, καὶ τέρπεται εὔκομα μῆλα,
καὶ ναῦται πλώουσι, Διώνυσος δὲ χορεύει,
καὶ μέλπει πετεεινά, καὶ ὠδίνουσι μέλισσαι,
πῶς οὐ χρὴ καὶ ἀοιδὸν ἐν εἴαρι καλὸν ἀεῖσαι;

Appendix

The poem on Spring, the Preface and Epilogue to the Garland

(9. 363)

Windy winter has left the sky, the bright [*or* purple] season of flower-bringing spring is smiling. The dark earth garlands herself with greenery [*lit.* green grass *or* foliage], and blossoming plants wave their new leaves. The meadows, drinking the soft dew of Dawn which nourishes plants, laugh as the roses open. [*7*] The shepherd in the hills is happy to play [shrilly] on his pipe, and the goatherd takes delight in the grey kids. Already sailors voyage over the broad waves, the Zephyr [*west wind*] swelling their sails with a kindly breeze. Already men shout 'Euai!' to Dionysos the grape-giver, crowning their hair with leaves of the berried ivy. [*13*] Bees born from bulls are concerned with their fine, artful works; sitting on the hive they build the fresh white beauties of the comb with many cells. Everywhere the race of birds sings loud and clear, kingfishers by the waves, swallows round houses, the swan by river-banks, the nightingale in the grove. [*19*] If the foliage of plants rejoices, and the earth is blooming, the shepherd playing the pipe, and the woolly flocks are happy, sailors sail and Dionysos dances, and the birds sing and bees reproduce, how should a singer too not sing finely in the spring?

If the poem is Meleager's, it is his only departure from elegiac couplets; the metre is the dactylic hexameter. The traditional ascription to Meleager was upheld by Geffcken and Reitzenstein, and recently by T. B. L. Webster, though rejected by others including Stadtmüller, who suggested Nikander as a possible author.

For the belief in the origin of bees, cf. Vergil's Fourth *Georgic*, 554 ff. – '... a miracle sudden and strange to tell of/They behold: from the oxen's bellies all over their rotting flesh/Creatures are humming, swarming through the wreckage of their ribs –/Huge and trailing clouds of bees, ...' (tr. C. Day Lewis).

Μοῦσα φίλα, τίνι τάνδε φέρεις πάγκαρπον ἀοιδάν,
ἢ τίς ὁ καὶ τεύξας ὑμνοθετᾶν στέφανον;
ἄνυσε μὲν Μελέαγρος, ἀριζάλῳ δὲ Διοκλεῖ
μναμόσυνον ταύταν ἐξεπόνησε χάριν,
5 πολλὰ μὲν ἐμπλέξας Ἀνύτης κρίνα, πολλὰ δὲ Μοιροῦς
λείρια, καὶ Σαπφοῦς βαιὰ μὲν ἀλλὰ ῥόδα,
νάρκισσόν τε τορῶν Μελανιππίδου ἔγκυον ὕμνων,
καὶ νέον οἰνάνθης κλῆμα Σιμωνίδεω,
σὺν δ' ἀναμὶξ πλέξας μυρόπνουν εὐάνθεμον ἶριν
10 Νοσσίδος, ἧς δέλτοις κηρὸν ἔτηξεν Ἔρως·
τῇ δ' ἅμα καὶ σάμψυχον ἀφ' ἡδυπνόοιο Ῥιανοῦ,
καὶ γλυκὺν Ἠρίννης παρθενόχρωτα κρόκον,
Ἀλκαίου τε λάληθρον ἐν ὑμνοπόλοις ὑάκινθον,
καὶ Σαμίου δάφνης κλῶνα μελαμπέταλον.
15 ἐν δὲ Λεωνίδεω θαλεροὺς κισσοῖο κορύμβους,
Μνασάλκου τε κόμας ὀξυτόρου πίτυος,
†βλαισήν τε πλατάνιστον ἀπέθρισε Παμφίλου οἴνης†
σύμπλεκτον καρύης ἔρνεσι Παγκράτεος,
Τύμνεώ τ' εὐπέταλον λεύκην, χλοερόν τε σίσυμβρον
20 Νικίου, Εὐφήμου τ' ἀμμότροφον πάραλον·
ἐν δ' ἄρα Δαμάγητον, ἴον μέλαν, ἡδύ τε μύρτον
Καλλιμάχου στυφελοῦ μεστὸν ἀεὶ μέλιτος,
λυχνίδα τ' Εὐφορίωνος, ἰδ' †ἐν Μούσῃσιν ἄμεινον†,
ὃς Διὸς ἐκ κούρων ἔσχεν ἐπωνυμίην.
25 τῆσι δ' ἅμ' Ἡγήσιππον ἐνέπλεκε, μαινάδα βότρυν,
Πέρσου τ' εὐώδη σχοῖνον ἀμησάμενος,
σὺν δ' ἅμα καὶ γλυκύμηλον ἀπ' ἀκρεμόνων Διοτίμου,
καὶ ῥοιῆς ἄνθη πρῶτα Μενεκράτεος,
μυρραίους τε κλάδους Νικαινέτου, ἠδὲ Φαέννου
30 τέρμινθον, βλωθρήν τ' ἀχράδα Σιμίεω·
ἐν δὲ καὶ ἐκ λειμῶνος ἀμωμήτοιο σέλινα
βαιὰ διακνίζων ἄνθεα Παρθενίδος,

(I, 4.1)

Dear Muse, to whom are you bringing these varied fruits of song; who was it made this garland of poets? – It was Meleager's doing; he worked at this, to present it as a memento to the excellent Diokles. [5] He inwove many of Anyte's lilies, and many by Moiro; few by Sappho, but they are roses; narcissi pregnant with the clear songs of Melanippides, and a fresh shoot of Simonides' vine-blossom; to mix with them he twined the spice-scented flowering iris of Nossis, on whose writing-tablets Love melted the wax [*the wax is softened by Eros' fire because Nossis wrote mainly love-poetry*]. [11] And with her, marjoram from sweet-breathing Rhianos, and Erinna's delicious crocus, with a girl's complexion [*she died aged nineteen*]; Alkaios's hyacinth, which is vocal to poets [*'Meleager perhaps means that the markings on the petals had no significance until poets fitted a word to them and made the flower vocal' – Gow and Page*]; and a dark-leaved branch of the bay-tree of Samios. [15] He inwove too Leonidas' [*of Tarentum*] fresh ivy-berries, and the sharp needles of Mnasalkes' pine; he gathered from the twisted tendrils of Pamphilos' vine, woven together with Pankrates' hazel-nuts; the fine-leaved white poplar of Tymnes, the green mint of Nikias, the spurge of Euphemos that grows on the sand; Damagetos the dark violet too, and Kallimachos' sweet myrtle, always full of astringent honey; Euphorion's rose-campion, and the cyclamen skilled in poetry whose name comes from the sons of Zeus [*the Dioskouroi – i.e. the poet is Dioskorides*]. [25] With them he inwove Hegesippos, an intoxicating bunch of grapes; the scented ginger-grass of Perses which he had cut, with a quince from the boughs of Diotimos, and the first pomegranate-flowers of Menekrates; twigs of Nikainetos' myrrh, the terebinth of Phaënnos, and the tall wild pear-tree of Simias. [31] From the fine meadow he took and distributed in small batches the flowers of Parthenis, celery; and yellow ears from Bakchylides' corn-stalks, fruitful gleanings from his honey-dropping Muse. [35] And Anakreon, whose sweet lyric song is of nectar, but a bloom which cannot be transplanted into elegiacs [*most of Anakreon's verse was lyric, and therefore disqualified from Meleager's anthology of poems in elegiac metre*]; a curly-leaved thistle-blossom from Archilochos' fodder – a few drops from the ocean [*epigrams form the smallest part of Archilochos' work*].

λείψανά τ' εὐκαρπεῦντα μελιστάκτων ἀπὸ Μουσέων
  ξανθοὺς ἐκ καλάμης Βακχυλίδεω στάχυας,
35 ἐν δ' ἄρ' Ἀνακρείοντα, τὸ μὲν γλυκὺ κεῖνο μέλισμα
  νέκταρος, εἰς δ' ἐλέγους ἄσπορον ἀνθέμιον,
ἐν δὲ καὶ ἐκ φορβῆς σκολιότριχος ἄνθος ἀκάνθης
  Ἀρχιλόχου, μικρὰς στράγγας ἀπ' ὠκεανοῦ,
τοῖς δ' ἅμ' Ἀλεξάνδροιο νέους ὀρπηκας ἐλαίης,
40   ἠδὲ Πολυκλείτου πορφυρέην κύαμον.
ἐν δ' ἄρ' ἀμάρακον ἧκε, Πολυστράτου ἄνθος ἀοιδῶν,
  Φοίνισσάν τε νέην κύπρον ἀπ' Ἀντιπάτρου.
καὶ μὴν καὶ Συρίαν σταχυότριχα θήκατο νάρδον,
  ὑμνοθέταν Ἑρμοῦ δῶρον ἀειδόμενον,
45 ἐν δὲ Ποσείδιππόν τε καὶ Ἡδύλον, ἄγρι' ἀρούρης,
  Σικελίδεώ τ' ἀνέμοις ἄνθεα φυόμενα.
ναὶ μὴν καὶ χρύσειον ἀεὶ θείοιο Πλάτωνος
  κλῶνα, τὸν ἐξ ἀρετῆς πάντοθι λαμπόμενον,
ἄστρων τ' ἴδριν Ἄρατον ὁμοῦ βάλεν, οὐρανομάκευς
50 φοίνικος κείρας πρωτογόνους ἕλικας,
λωτόν τ' εὐχαίτην Χαιρήμονος, ἐν φλογὶ μίξας
  Φαιδίμου, Ἀνταγόρου τ' εὔστροφον ὄμμα βοός,
τάν τε φιλάκρητον Θεοδωρίδεω νεοθαλῆ
  ἕρπυλλον, κυάνων τ' ἄνθεα Φανίεω,
55 ἄλλων τ' ἔρνεα πολλὰ νεόγραφα, τοῖς δ' ἅμα Μούσης
  καὶ σφετέρης ἔτι που πρώιμα λευκόια.
ἀλλὰ φίλοις μὲν ἐμοῖσι φέρω χάριν· ἔστι δὲ μύσταις
  κοινὸς ὁ τῶν Μουσέων ἡδυεπὴς στέφανος.

[39] With them Alexander's young olive-shoots, and the crimson bean-plant of Polykleitos. He put marjoram, the flower of Polystratos' songs, with them, and fresh Phoenician henna from Antipater [*of Sidon*]; he added Syrian spikenard, the poet we sing of as 'the gift of Hermes' [*i.e. Hermodoros*]; and the wild flowers of the corn-field, Poseidippos and Hedylos, and the anemones of Sikelidas [*the name by which both Theokritos and Hedylos also call Asklepiades*]. [48] Yes, and the golden branch of the ever-divine Plato, everywhere bright with his skill; together with Aratos who knew the stars [*he wrote the astronomical and meteorological poem 'Phainomena'*], cutting the first-grown branches from his heaven-high palm-tree. And Chairemon's finely-petalled lotus, mixed with the wall-flower of Phaidimos, and Antagoras' finely-turning ox-eyes, Theodoridas' sprouting, wine-loving thyme [*thyme was perhaps an ingredient of garlands worn at symposia*], and Phanias' corn-flowers; [55] and many recently-written buds of others, together with these early snowdrops of his own Muse. I bring the gift to my friends, but the Muses' garland of sweet words is the common property of all the initiated.

Meleager's preface to his *Garland*. Nothing is known of the Diokles to whom he dedicates the collection. Of the forty-seven poets named as contributors, all except four – Melanippides, Euphemos, Parthenis and Polykleitos – have epigrams extant in The Greek Anthology. Meleager was always fond of flower-metaphors and imagery, but the association of flowers with poetry was far from new. The order of contents in Meleager's listing of the poets is fairly haphazard, and it is difficult to discern any critical point in the application of most of the plants to their poets – though the tags on Sappho, Archilochos and Kallimachos are apt enough. The version follows Gow and Page's suggestion that in line 17 'πλατάνιστον conceals some word meaning "tendril" or the like, or has that unrecorded sense itself.' In line 23 I translate *exempli gratia* εὔμουσον κυκλάμινον.

Ἁ πύματον καμπτῆρα καταγγέλλουσα κορωνίς,
 ἑρκοῦρος γραπταῖς πιστοτάτα σελίσιν.
φαμὶ τὸν ἐκ πάντων ἠθροισμένον εἰς ἕνα μόχθον
 ὑμνοθετᾶν βύβλῳ τᾷδ' ἐνελιξάμενον
ἐκτελέσαι Μελέαγρον, ἀείμνηστον δὲ Διοκλεῖ
 ἄνθεσι συμπλέξαι μουσοπόλον στέφανον.
οὖλα δ' ἐγὼ καμφθεῖσα δρακοντείοις ἴσα νώτοις
 σύνθρονος ἵδρυμαι τέρμασιν εὐμαθίας.

(CXXIX, 12.257)

I, the colophon announcing the last turning-point [*start of the last lap*], most faithful watchman of the written columns [*i.e. pages*], I announce that Meleager has finished, he who rolled up in this book the work [*same metaphorical sense*] of all the poets, gathered into one; and that he plaited with flowers this ever-to-be-remembered garland of poetry [*lit.* Muse-serving garland] for Diokles. Curled twistedly like the back of a snake, I am settled [here], enthroned at the limits of this learned work [*lit.* well-learning].

The second poem specially composed for the publication of the *Garland* – this time to conclude it. The last two lines describe the actual *koronis* or colophon, the device drawn to mark the end of the manuscript.

A Note on Garlands, Symposia and the Komos

The symposion was an important feature of Greek social life. The word means roughly 'drinking-party', but it was rather a whole evening of social and intellectual entertainment. It was originally an occasion for young men, attended by girl musicians, taking place in the *andrōn* (a specially decorated and furnished men's suite) of the host's house. Its ingredients were music played by the flute-girls, cabaret performances, drinking-songs (*skolia*), poetry reading and impromptu verse by the guests – and above all, discussions of a general, philosophic or literary kind, sometimes on specific agreed topics (as in the Socratic kind of symposion).

The nature of the symposion occasioned a minor literary genre. Works such as the *Symposion* of Plato, those of Xenophon and Plutarch and the *Deipnosophistai* ('Scholars at Dinner') of Athenaios employ the framework of the symposion as a formal basis for different kinds of dialogue.

In the early third century BC collections of epigrams were made which derived partly from the symposion. Many of the poems were literary versions of the sort of extempore poems, riddles, etc. improvised at symposia. Asklepiades is a master of this kind of poem, which was to give a new direction to epigram in the early Hellenistic period. T. B. L. Webster, in *Hellenistic Poetry and Art* (1964), shows how the ambience of the symposion was used by the third-century poets Asklepiades, Poseidippos, Hedylos and Kallimachos. The classic study of poetry connected with the symposion is R. Reitzenstein's *Epigramm und Skolion* (1893).

Garlands were worn at symposia, and at the *kōmos* which sometimes ensued. At the symposion the fading garland was thought to be the sign of an unlucky lover, as in these lines of Kallimachos (AP 12.134)–

> Our guest's wound went unnoticed. Didn't you see him
> Dragging breath painfully from his lungs
> As he drank the third cup? And the roses

Taking leave of his garland, dropping their petals
Over the floor? . . .
[tr. Peter Jay]

As a decorative motif in art, the garland of mixed flowers goes back even further than the Hellenistic period in which it becomes fairly common.

Kōmos has two main senses – the general one of 'revel, carousal, merry-making', and the concrete sense of 'a band of revellers' (Liddell and Scott, who give examples of its use by Pindar for the procession which preceded a victor in athletic games; and of its use by Euripides for any group of people – e.g. of an army, of hunters, etc.). But there is the sense – almost amounting to a technical term – common in the epigrammatists, which is not noted by Liddell and Scott, to which Walter Headlam devotes a long note in *The Mimes of Herodas*. I quote from his note on Herodas 2.34, omitting his exhaustive mass of references:

> One of the most picturesque features of Greek and Roman life [was] the practice of young men in the evening after their wine (when sufficiently drunk), sallying forth alone or in bands *epi kōmon*, *comissatum*, accompanied sometimes with flute-girls, to the houses of friends, . . . usually of women with the garlands they had worn already at dessert, and pipes, and torches. They would beg to be admitted, singing a serenade *paraklausithyron* [song sung at the mistress' door – ed.], a form of *aulēsis* [flute-song – ed.] accompanied by a dance. . . . The lover's object was of course to advise the lady of his presence: and, in order to attract her attention more effectually, he would knock at the door. At Athens, we know this to have been a punishable offence, under what conditions does not appear, but the kind of annoyance that might be caused by unchecked horseplay is indicated by Appul. *De Mag.* 75 ['*her house became wholly like a brothel . . . stones thrown by youthful pranksters battered her doors day and night, the windows rattled all round with their songs, and the dining-room was rowdy with serenaders*' – ed.]
>
> If the lady chose to exclude him, *apokleiein*, the lover would linger at the door, hang his wreath upon it, leave his burnt-out torch, or lie down upon the ground and wait, not of course omitting to inform his mistress. . . . Fights often took place between rivals, and the result of such a brawl might be the bursting open of the door, but the desperate lover would often threaten to force the door or burn it out of his own impatience, . . . and there are stories enough to show that it was not unfrequently done. We

read of a girl carried off [*here he refers to Meleager, poem 45*], of a man who *epekōmasen* [went serenading] to carry off a boy....

Four poems by Asklepiades illustrating the *kōmos*-theme are AP 5.64, 5.145, 5.164 and 5.167.

Select Bibliography

This does not include all the works referred to by their authors' names in the Notes. For these and a full textual bibliography see the 'List of Texts Consulted' in Gow and Page's *Hellenistic Epigrams*.

TEXTS AND COMMENTARIES

F. Graefe   *Meleagri Gadareni Epigrammata*, 1811
K. Radinger   *Meleagros von Gadara*, 1895
W. R. Paton   *The Greek Anthology*, 5 vols., 1916. Text (unreliable) and prose versions of the complete Palatine Anthology and Planudean Appendix.
A. S. F. Gow and D. L. Page   *Hellenistic Epigrams*, 2 vols. (text and commentary), 1965. An important edition of all the epigrammatists from the time of Asklepiades to Meleager.

STUDIES OF MELEAGER

C. A. Sainte-Beuve   *Méléagre*, 1845. A lengthy essay, collected in *Portraits Contemporains*, vol. V.
H. Ouvré   *Méléagre de Gadara*, 1894. The only book-length study entirely devoted to Meleager.

GENERAL

R. Reitzenstein   *Epigramm und Skolion*, 1893
J. W. Mackail   *Select Epigrams from The Greek Anthology*, 3rd edition, 1911. The Introduction is a useful study of Greek epigram.
J. A. Symonds   *Studies of the Greek Poets*, 3rd edition, 1920. Includes some of Symonds' verse translations.
A. Körte   *Hellenistic Poetry*, translated by Jacob Hammer and Moses Hadas, 1929

A. Couat *Alexandrian Poetry*, translated by James Loeb, 1931

T. B. L. Webster *Hellenistic Poetry and Art*, 1964. An excellent study of the history of poetry during the period up to and including Meleager.

TRANSLATIONS

Walter Headlam *Fifty Poems of Meleager*, 1890. Bilingual text with a brief preface. Headlam later disowned the work.

Richard Aldington *The Poems of Meleager of Gadara*, 1920. Prose versions with a brief preface but no notes or references.

F. A. Wright *The Complete Poems of Meleager of Gadara*, 1924. Noteworthy as perhaps the feeblest verse translation of any ancient poet.

Frederick Baron Corvo, with Sholto Douglas *The Songs of Meleager*, 1937. Greek texts and highly erratic prose versions which 'halt between the literal and the aesthetick' (sic). The mistaking of Kos for Keos, an island nearly 200 miles to the west, is a trivial error in this context.

www.ingramcontent.com/pod-product-compliance
Lightning Source LLC
Chambersburg PA
CBHW021714230426
43668CB00008B/832